The New HR Leader's *First 100 Days*

How To Start Strong, Hit The Ground Running & ACHIEVE SUCCESS FASTER As A NEW Human Resources Manager, Director or VP

The 15 PROVEN Rules You Must Follow

Alan Collins

Success in HR Publishing
Chicago, Illinois USA

Dedicated to my son, Bryan.

Fifty percent of the proceeds of this book will
go to the Bryan A. Collins Memorial Scholarship Program
which provides scholarships to deserving, high potential
minority students who excel in academics and in
service to others. I encourage you to join me in
supporting this truly worthwhile cause at
www.BryanCollinsScholarship.org.

— CONTENTS —

HR Career Success Resources
by Alan Collins

HR INTERVIEW SECRETS:
How To Ace Your Next Human
Resources Interview, Dazzle Your
Interviewers & LAND THE JOB
YOU WANT!

Available now at:
www.HRInterviewSecrets.com

HR RESUME SECRETS:
How To Create An Irresistible
Human Resources Resume That Will
Open Doors, Wow Hiring Managers
& Get You Interviews!

Available now at:
www.HRResumeSecrets.com

UNWRITTEN HR RULES:
21 Secrets for Attaining
Awesome Career Success
in Human Resources

Available now at:
www.UnwrittenHRRules.com

More HR Career Success Resources
By Alan Collins

BEST KEPT HR SECRETS:
400 Most Powerful Tips For Thriving
At Work, Making Yourself Indispensa-
ble & Attaining Outrageous Success in
Human Resources

Available now at:
www.BestKeptHRSecrets.com

STAY INSPIRED IN HR:
21 Positive Reminders To
Keep You Motivated, Encouraged,
Confident & Committed To
Success in Human Resources!

Available now at:
www.StayInspiredInHR.com

WINNING BIG IN HR:
100+ Powerful Strategies For
Accomplishing Great Results Faster &
Getting Your Clients To Rave About
You As A Human Resources
Professional!
Available now at:
www.WinningBigInHR.com

Introduction
THE #1 REASON HR LEADERS FAIL

Congratulations on landing your new HR leadership role! I'm sure you're excited and can't wait to get started.

Now, let me tell you something you may not want to hear…

According to extensive research done by SHRM (Society of Human Resources Management), 31% of new HR leaders FAIL in their first 12-18 months.

Sadly, most are either fired or just leave on their own.

Of those few "failures" given a second chance to remain in their organizations, all operate under intense pressure to get their act together fast, or they'll be on the street too. Unfortunately, many of them ultimately don't make it either.

What's the reason for these failures?

Is it trouble figuring out the new culture?

Is it not winning over their team?

Is it not wowing their clients?

Is it not delivering results?

Is it not making their mark fast enough?

Yes, those are all important contributing factors.

However, the <u>#1 REASON</u> is much more subtle and traces back to the beginning when they <u>did not START STRONG</u> – did <u>not take charge</u> of their precious 90 to 100-day honeymoon period, made <u>bad early decisions</u> producing missed expectations – ultimately causing their derailment.

Even for successful new HR leaders that do survive beyond their second year, their success is powerfully determined by the **decisions and choices made in their crucial <u>first</u> <u>few</u> <u>months.</u>**

So don't underestimate the beginning of your tenure in any HR leadership position. It is one of the toughest and riskiest periods of your career, no matter how much experience you have.

What makes it so difficult? Well, for one, I hate to burst your bubble, but you cannot rely on your boss or the organization to onboard, train, or prepare you for your new role.

Most bosses, while obviously invested in your success, are stretched thin, busy as hell, and don't have time to hold your hand. And frankly, this shouldn't surprise you.

YOU are expected to hit the ground running. YOU are expected to STEP UP and establish yourself in the organization. YOU are expected to proactively close any knowledge gaps. YOU are expected to learn the culture, navigate the politics and build relationships. YOU are expected to deliver the results expected.

All of this is on YOU. It's on your shoulders to take charge and figure this out. Why? Because you're a leader, and that's what you're being PAID to do!

That said, all this can be daunting, especially if you're making a big career step up, confused about what to do first...or if you lack a roadmap.

However, relax. You got this.

This book is your <u>ROADMAP.</u>

It specifically provides...

15 Proven Rules To Help You Start Strong, Hit The Ground Running & Guide You To Success Faster

Whether you're an HR Manager moving into your first leadership position...or a newly promoted Director in the talent management arena...or an experienced HR VP in a Fortune 100 company, <u>these</u> <u>rules</u> <u>work.</u> They're proven, validated and supported by in-depth conversations with successful HR leaders across all types of organizations – and will enable you to get up to speed quickly and accelerate your move into your new role.

Consider what you're reading as a one-of-a-kind, underground playbook developed just for HR professionals that will help you effectively manage your leadership transition.

That said, before we get started, let's talk about...

How To Squeeze The Most Juice From These Pages

I recommend two strategies for going through the 15 rules in this book:

1. **Scanner method:** Quickly flip through this book from front to back. The major tips and strategies have been **bolded and highlighted** to jump out and grab your attention. Mark the most important ideas you like first and then go back to deep dive into them later.

2. **Sniper method:** If you've already started in your new role and know where you need to focus most, simply jump to that specific Rule and focus on those tactics. The **Summary & Action Steps** at the end of each of the 15 rules will recap specifically what you should do.

Once you've finished either 1 or 2, then **start putting together your own Onboarding Plan (see Rule #2).** Do this by listing 5-7 specific items from this book you want to take action on immediately. Then add more action items to your list as the old ones get checked off and as you grow into your new role. This is what will put you well ahead of the game.

A caveat: Everything you read in this book won't be applicable or a top priority. The information most relevant will depend on if you're a new HR leader promoted from within or a new hire from the outside. The good thing is that you'll know right away what fits your situation and what doesn't.

You'll want to keep this book with you for your entire HR career. It will serve as your personal coach to ensure that each time you change HR jobs, you can do so in a way that will accelerate your success.

This book is all about results – and getting them in the fastest way possible – and with the least amount of stress and frustration.

Now let's begin by making sure you start strong and hit the ground running!

Sincerely,

Alan Collins

Alan L. Collins
Founder, Success in HR

*   *   *

Rule #1:

CHEAT IF YOU WANT TO START STRONG & HIT THE GROUND RUNNING

HR Magazine offered this sage bit of advice in a recent issue: **"The transition into a new HR leadership role should begin the <u>moment</u> you accept the job offer."** They were quoting a key conclusion from a major SHRM onboarding study.

The rationale?

They argued strongly, and I agree that at the end of 90 to 100 days (or roughly one business quarter), your "honeymoon period" is over...*whether you officially have one or not!* And the key people, namely your boss, clients, and direct reports, all expect you to be making an <u>impact.</u>

And for you, therein lies a dirty little secret for getting off to an explosively positive start in your new role...

> **Don't play fair! CHEAT...by starting your transition well <u>BEFORE</u> you officially arrive on day one.**

Think about it. One hundred days isn't a heck of a lot of time to get up to speed, take charge, build your team, and get results. So if you want an edge, start taking concrete actions to prepare for your new job sooner than anyone expects you to – which is right after you say "YES!" to the offer. Doing this simply gives you more time to ready yourself to hit the ground running.

How much time should you take between jobs to prepare? If you're changing employers, **two weeks** (or more) minimum. Less won't work. You need time to get your act together first.

Here are **five actions** you should consider taking to capitalize on this valuable **pre-start period.**

Action#1:
Take Time to Disconnect
From the Old Job.

This is crucial! Make a clean break. Cut the old cord as quickly as possible.

Don't waste time calling back to your old gig to ensure everything is running fine (it may not be, but it's not your problem). Don't ask if they miss you (they might, but they'll survive). Don't ask if the place is falling apart without you (it may be, but someone will step in and pick up the pieces).

Here's the sad truth: in a few months, no one will notice you're gone.

Instead, shake off your old job immediately. Take a break and start getting ready for your new one. **Hopping right into a brand new HR leadership challenge without pausing piles on more stress exactly when you need to start fresh.**

Remember, once you start in a new organization, you may not be able to take another vacation for a while. So consider using this gap between jobs to take a "reset" vacation so you begin rested and de-stressed. This could be a week wandering in the woods, biking, shopping your brains out, getting a week of sleep at home...or taking some weeks for exotic travel. Anything to relax you and take the edge off.

Action #2:
Get A Jumpstart On Your Major
Onboarding Priorities.

Use this precious pre-start period to get a head start on **high-payback activities** that will help you make a smoother transition into your new role – such as:

1. Prioritizing your key influencers (Action #3 below).

2. Building relationships early (Action #4 below).
3. Drafting your own Onboarding Plan (see Rule #2).
4. Deepening your knowledge of the business and how your role fits (see Rule #3).

No matter what kind of HR leadership role you're moving into, these are the absolute essentials. **So start grinding through this shortlist <u>as soon as possible</u>...*even if you can't get them all done before day one.*** These are your essential job-related priorities.

Action #3:
Prioritize Your Key Influencers.

Key influencers are those people who can **directly <u>influence</u> and <u>impact</u> your performance, your success, and how you are perceived in the organization.** Therefore, building successful relationships with these people is crucial in your first 100 days.
They include the following:

- **Higher-ups:** This group, of course, includes your direct boss. But also your indirect (or dotted-line) boss if there is a matrix organization, your boss's boss, your boss's assistant, or anyone else that resides further up in the organization's food chain who is important to your performance or how you're viewed. If you're in the top HR job in a public company, this also includes the Board of Directors.

- **Clients:** This group includes the business leaders and their teams that you'll be supporting with your HR advice, insights, and services. For example, if you are in a manufacturing site, it would be that location's Plant Manager and her direct reports. If you're in a global HR leadership role, it would be all the countries or regional business leaders who have P&L accountability for those locations – and their teams.

- **Direct reports:** These are the associates or team members that report directly to you. However, you'll want to pay particular attention to those folks on your team who are *high performers* or *retention risks*. This group could also include dotted line direct reports if you reside in a matrix organization -- as well as other critical support people who reside below your level in the organization but who nevertheless will help you carry out your key HR initiatives.

- **Key Colleagues:** These are vital peers, allies, and even the person who wanted your job but didn't get it. Suppose you're in an HR generalist leadership role. In that case, your key colleagues include the functional specialists in Talent Acquisition, Total Rewards, HRIS, Organization Development, and the like that support or provide services to you and your clients. If you're in an HR specialist leadership role, your key colleagues include the HR generalists and the client organization you support in your area of the business.

Depending on your role, there may be many people in these groups. **However, don't make the mistake of thinking that everyone is an influencer.** *They're not.* You can't satisfy or develop deep relationships with everybody. So don't try.

Instead, you should…

Narrow Your List of Influencers
If your list is huge, you should chunk it down to those people *absolutely essential* to your success. However, since you're a newbie, making a complete list of these individuals can be a head-scratcher. Some key influencers will be obvious. Others could be buried within the bowels of the organization, like hibernating bears, and not so apparent. So get some help in compiling and prioritizing your list. Get org charts and utilize your boss. Talk to your recruiter. Tap into a trusted internal colleague to help you.

If you're not certain if someone is a key influencer, keep them on your list anyway until you're sure they're not. Neglecting a key influencer can be tough to recover from and can have a disastrous effect on your ability to make a smooth transition.

Here's What Happened to a Total Rewards Director Who Failed to Heed This Warning.

Matt, a former colleague of mine, was hired to head up compensation and benefits for a medium-sized division of an oil company. With his boss' help, he reviewed the org charts, mapped out his key influencers, and began building relationships with them.

However, shortly after that, the Compensation Director of a different division began undermining Matt's work with the Corporate Total Rewards group -- a department they both reported to on a dotted-line basis.

Matt did not understand why his cross-divisional counterpart was working against him since he had never met her.

It turned out she was miffed that he hadn't seen her as important enough to call or establish a relationship with. Previously, she had bonded well with his predecessor, enjoying their weekly chats about comp policy and company gossip. She had hoped to establish the same relationship with Matt – except no one told him.

Instead, unknowingly, he overlooked her when he compiled his list of key influencers to connect with. She saw this as a sign of disrespect, and Matt created an unwarranted rift with her that took him months to resolve.

Don't stumble as Matt did.

Avoid locking down your list too soon.

Ask questions and dig deep to flush out all your potential influencers. Then edit your list as you move through the organization and get to know where people fit.

Once you've identified and narrowed your influencers, then it's time to…

Scope Them Out Online

Use LinkedIn, Facebook and Google as your primary research tools. Find out everything there is to know about these folks – especially those you'll be interacting with on a regular basis.

In particular, spend time studying their LinkedIn profile pages like you've never had anything better to do in your life.

- Did you attend the same school?
- Do you have common outside interests?
- Do you have common life events (e.g., kids and pets)?

Do this before you meet them. Since many have already checked you out online (or will soon), turnabout is fair play.

You want to use this information subtly. You don't want to say: "Oh, I looked you up on Linkedin and saw that we share an interest in..." That's how you go from new leader to stalker.

Instead, use this info to help you prepare potential conversation starters with the people you meet that you'll only use if they're brought up first by them -- through cues they drop in conversation, pictures on their wall, items on their desk, or commonly known tidbits mentioned by others.

Action #4:
Build Relationships Early.

This one strategy is absolutely pure gold. Essentially it boils down to...

Doing As Many Meet & Greets As Humanly
Possible -- Before You Arrive.

After your offer acceptance, get your boss' approval to immediately connect with your direct reports and other key influencers *minimally by phone* before your official first day.

While this may not be appropriate in all cases, in situations when your arrival is well-known, your new boss will be thrilled that you want to get a head start.

In talking with each person, introduce yourself and let them know how excited you are to be joining the team. At a minimum, in your chats, you'll want to:

- **Gather info about them:** Ask casual questions about their role, background, tenure with the organization, and the key priorities they're working against.
- **Get their advice about your role:** Specifically, "What would you suggest I do to thrive as a new HR leader in this organization?" and "What do you think my team needs from me to succeed?"
- **Finally, reiterate your enthusiasm about the job** and your desire to know them better once you arrive.

This small effort to reach out, introduce yourself and learn more about your key influencers (and their priorities) will set a positive tone before day one and give you a considerable edge.

Here's a Story I'll Never Forget That Illustrates the Power of Reaching Out To Your Key Influencers Before Your First Day.

Deon Riley came into our organization from the outside as a new HR director in our Gatorade division, reporting to me. Her key clients included seven plant managers – four of whom she talked with during her interviews.

However, a week before she started, she still had not met three of them. So, anticipating a problem, I indicated to her that, politically, it was essential that she connect with ALL of them. (We wanted no one feeling left out and holding it against her even before she had a chance to get out of the starting gate.)

She immediately called each of them that week, introduced herself personally, asked them about their biggest challenges, and expressed her enthusiasm about meeting them in person soon.

But then she proactively went beyond this.

With my blessing, she decided before her arrival that she should also talk to her three direct reports and two peers in Compensation and Labor Relations. She would need their support, too, as she was anticipating key HR initiatives that she would be leading involving these areas.

The result: Her clients, direct reports, and peers were all blown away by her desire to build relationships before meeting them officially. As a result, when she arrived, everyone felt like she'd already been there forever. They admired her passion, curiosity, and sincerity.

And after 100 days, Deon was seen as a clear high potential and future senior HR leader.

Since then, this has proved accurate as she has gone on to bigger and better things serving as the SVP of HR at Abercrombie & Fitch and Ross Stores.

Learn from Deon's example.

Don't hesitate to set up these types of pre-arrival meetings. You might expect to encounter resistance, but this rarely happens. In fact, many leaders appreciate talking with newcomers to the organization. Some regard it as "reverse onboarding" – where they tap into your fresh "outsider" insights about the company and the industry.

Nevertheless, to make your early discussions easier and flow naturally, **develop some conversation starters.** Here are a few examples:

"Hi Scott, I'm Ramona. I'll be starting next week as the new HR manager supporting the Global Marketing team. Jennifer told me that you're an absolutely vital member of that team. I didn't want to show up without getting a chance to chat with you in advance...."

"Kelly, since you were traveling the day I was in for interviews, we haven't met. But I'd love to spend some time with you before I start..."

"Morgan, since you're such a key member of our team, I can't imagine starting my first day without getting to know you first. I'd love to meet you for coffee whenever and wherever is most

convenient for you, in the next couple of days. I'd really love to get your insights, specifically on the XYZ restructuring initiative, before I start."

Frankly, not everyone may not have time to reach out and connect with you. But if you can make this happen – with even just a few people – you'll lay a phenomenal foundation before your first day.

This is the time you are making many critical first impressions. So carefully plan and prepare for these meetings with key influencers. Perceptions of you and your behaviors are being set. So it would be best if you were the one to script them.

Speaking of scripting, you should also script an <u>introduction</u> and <u>elevator pitch</u> to facilitate these discussions.

Here's an example:

A brief introduction...
Hi Raul, I'm Sue Cohen. It's great meeting you!

If needed, here's a brief elevator pitch...
I'm the new HR director in the E-commerce division. Before I started here a few days ago, I was with Netflix for three years in their Talent Management group. I worked there on initiatives to help attract and develop their top marketing talent. Looking forward to doing the same here.

That's it. That's all you need. Once you've introduced yourself, quickly pivot back to their favorite topic: *themselves.* You're in a learning period, so you want to gather as much info as possible about them. If the conversation shifts back to you, anticipate the kinds of questions you think you will be asked about the HR work you were hired to do. Also, what types of things you enjoy doing away from work? Craft <u>concise</u> answers to those questions and <u>practice</u> responding to them.

Use this intro/elevator pitch during your first few weeks or until your story changes to reflect your new job. You'll find this useful for pre-start discussions and during your early days on the job when you'll meet other folks in planned (or unplanned) situations.

Action #5:
If You're Relocating, Address Needs At Your Home Base.

You can make the case that this should be at the top of your pre-start list. And I wouldn't disagree with you – especially if you're relocating and a family is involved.

In this case, poor planning on the home front can distract you from focusing adequate time establishing yourself at work. For this reason alone, it may be worthwhile to buy yourself a few extra days, weeks, or more before you officially start. If you are moving, you can use this time **to list out and execute against your home base priorities** -- for example:

- Getting your home office set up with your wi-fi, computers, phones, files, and other needed resources.
- Having utility services such as gas, electricity, cable TV, and Internet connections turned off at your previous home and turned on in your new home on moving day.
- Making sure you have stocked up on all prescriptions and getting copies of any medical records you need to provide to your new doctors (including your veterinarian).
- Filling out change-of-address cards at your local post office.
- Notifying credit card companies, banks, creditors, and other important contacts of your new address.
- Transferring funds and arranging check cashing in your new hometown.
- Figuring out where extra help is needed -- meal delivery, relocation assistance, errand services, etc.
- And hundreds of other little yet essential things.

If you have a family, there's even more to consider, as you're not the only one making a transition. *They are transitioning*

as well. It takes time to figure out housing, schools, day care, transportation, etc.

This is further complicated if your spouse/partner is making a job transition too, and your children are leaving their friends, familiar communities and changing schools. Suddenly, your to-do list can become massive, emotionally draining, and a distraction that can undermine your ability to fully concentrate in your new HR role during your crucial early days.

Clearly, your family and the people you love are essential to your success in HR. And you want to get this right. So make sure you devote adequate time here.

To help ease the family's transition, here are some key pre-Start tips:

Get your spouse/partner's input on your start date. Depending on the challenges you anticipate facing on the job, it may make sense to collaborate on the timing of your first day. For example, together, you might decide that it makes sense to take that long-deferred vacation. Or instead, to get on the new employer's payroll and health insurance ASAP. Discuss how much time is needed to take care of work and family essentials and keep your relationship together intact -- when you know you'll have much less personal time to nurture it later.

Set a goal to re-establish your family's support system quickly. Relocating cuts ties with providers of needed services for your family – namely doctors, dentists, babysitters, tutors, and more. Assess your current network of providers, identify priorities and find replacements. Support from close relatives, such as grandparents, also can help fill needed gaps. Once you've done this, begin re-establishing familiar family rituals as quickly as possible and maintaining them throughout your transition.

Keep your spouse/partner positive and engaged. If they quit their old job to find a new one after relocating, anxiety and misery can erode the home front if their job search is slow. To speed up their progress, negotiate upfront with your company for spousal/partner job-search support or find such support shortly after moving. In any case, don't let your better half disengage or get depressed.

Max out your company's relocation services. Most company relocation services are limited to counseling, helping you buy/sell your home, moving belongings, and locating schools. While the counseling is good in many cases, don't hesitate to push back and request even more support for your family or ask them to direct you to employees who have recently relocated, who can provide advice on resources and shortcuts. In addition, if you are moving internationally, get professional advice about the cross-cultural transition. Isolation is an even greater risk for you and your family when language and cultural barriers exist.

Summary & Action Steps

Don't underestimate **what you need** and the **time** necessary to successfully transition as the new HR leader.

CHEAT by fully utilizing your valuable pre-start period to get rested and knock out the essentials before day one. That includes these **five actions**:

1. Disconnecting from the old job.
2. Getting a jumpstart on your major onboarding priorities.
3. Prioritizing your key influencers.
4. Building relationships early.
5. If you're relocating, address needs at your home base.

These are the key steps to take to enable you to make a smooth landing and get off to an accelerated start.

However, if you're pressed for time and can do nothing else, develop a **draft onboarding plan**, start building relationships with your key influencers, and **address your home base needs** as soon as you accept the offer. Delaying this will slow down your ability to get up to speed quickly.

* * *

Rule #2:
DEVELOP YOUR OWN HR
ONBOARDING PLAN

Envision this: you've now arrived on your first day.

You're the leader now. Everyone is watching, from your team members to your boss and peers. You want to start strong in your new role.

You're introduced around, grab a coffee and sit down for the first time. And then, after a few hours...Bam!

You're hit with a hurricane of demands.

- Suddenly you've got the head of marketing waiting to see you about replacing his best brand manager who just quit.
- You're handed a confidential envelope containing the fresh new sexual harassment charge your predecessor left you to handle.
- Your boss' assistant calls to remind you about the employee engagement presentation *you are already scheduled* to give in two days -- which you knew nothing about.

That's not all.

In the days that follow, you are confronted with ten other fires just like these waiting to be extinguished.

But don't people realize you've barely started?

You're a newbie, and you still need to get up to speed. Don't they know this?

How do you take charge in this situation?

Well, there are **two actions** that you should take simultaneously.

Action #1:
Fight Those Immediate Fires In A Way That Buys You Some Time.

Don't let yourself get caught up trying to extinguish every little blaze in your early days. Or get pressured to make crucial tough calls before you're ready.

On the other hand, let's be clear...

> **What you CANNOT DO is ignore or completely close yourself off from the inferno of HR issues currently facing the organization until you're 100% ready and fully onboarded.**

That won't work either.

The solution? You need to strike a balance.

That means you SHOULD jump in, grab a hose and fight those fires you absolutely can with <u>reasonable</u> <u>confidence.</u>

On the others, you need to **delegate** and **renegotiate,** which means specifically:

- If you have strong or experienced team members, you may want to delegate some items from your plate onto theirs temporarily. *(This is also a way to get an early read on their capabilities).*
- You may want to reschedule or re-negotiate deadlines with your clients.
- You may need your boss' help prioritizing and temporarily running interference on a couple of items.
- And yes, you may need to disappoint some people by saying no to *a few* low-priority requests. Or punting them to someone else in the organization. Or paying a consultant to do them for you. Or agreeing to do them but making it crystal clear they may not be done perfectly.

Again, all of these are **temporary tactics** to avoid being devoured by smoke and to allow you time to execute...

Action #2:
Schedule Blocks of Time to Execute
Your <u>Onboarding Plan.</u>

What's an onboarding plan? **The plan will ramp you up quickly, familiarize you with your new role, and allow you to take charge confidently.**

To further clarify, let me tell you what it is NOT. It's not the typical company-sponsored, one-day orientation *program.* You know, the one most companies run for all new employees. The one where a top business leader or CEO will kick it off with a state of the business. The one where HR covers policies, benefits, values, and culture. The one where Security will bore you to death covering space, facilities, and access. The one where some companies offer specific training on leadership or team building activities or executive-level welcome sessions.

While a program like this can be helpful and one you should attend, it's not nearly what you need.

Your specific onboarding plan is much more comprehensive and in-depth. But it shouldn't be complicated. **It can be a simple 1-2 page document that identifies key priorities and high-payback activities that will quickly get you up to speed.** For example, your plan might look like this:

1. Meet with your entire team on Day One to introduce yourself and to indicate that you'll be scheduling time to speak with them again *as a team* shortly when you have more to say.
2. Meet one-on-one with each of your direct reports within the first week. Send them your agenda for those meetings ahead of time.
3. Meet with your boss and other key business leaders and clients. Send them in advance your agenda for those discussions.
4. Coordinate with your admin, assistant, or chief of staff, if you're fortunate enough to have one. Assign them the *HR Onboarding Accelerator checklist* (see Rule #9). Request

that they pull the data, access the information and provide it to you.

5. Visit with reps in key departments that support your group. Examples: Finance, IT, Legal, Corporate Communications, and Security.

6. If you have them, meet with your finance rep and HRIS, and figure out how to access your team's financial reports and talent/workforce metrics for your client groups.

7. If you're the HR lead for a business unit, manufacturing location, or sales organization, immediately get on top of the numbers and key metrics. Then, meet with your finance lead or CFO to check your interpretation.

8. If you're making a giant leap into this role, engage a coach or mentor who can help you close any leadership or skill gaps.

9. Determine what significant HR company policies and practices you need to understand (i.e., the HRIS platform, the performance review system, the employee handbook, etc.).

10. Reach out to colleagues and key influencers you haven't met yet.

11. Learn the status and history of the vital HR initiatives you'll be responsible for.

12. Introduce yourself to crucial consultants or third-party HR vendors and get updated on their issues and priorities.

These are just example items to give you a flavor. Your own plan should be written, even if it just consists of bullet points. It should specify priorities and goals as well as milestones. You should share it with your boss and get buy-in for it. It should serve as a "contract" between the two of you, clarifying how you will spend your time.

All this comes down to the fact that you can easily get stretched in several directions. The essence of being an effective HR leader is prioritizing what's most essential to accelerate your success.

That's what your onboarding plan should do.

How Do You Come Up With Your Own Onboarding Plan?

1. **Start by tapping into your boss, key influencers, and predecessor in the role.** Get their advice on the most crucial initial onboarding activities you should engage in to quickly get you up to speed. Of course, you will also want to check in with your team once you come aboard officially.

2. **Refer to Best Practice Tool 2.1 provided at the end of this chapter as a model.** It's a *real onboarding plan* created by Jill Navarro. I've disguised the names to protect the guilty. This one covers 100 days, separated into 30-day increments, and was revised by Jill "about 20-25 times" during her onboarding period. It should give you another reference point for putting your own plan together.

   Caution: Make sure your plan addresses *your* needs and is customized to *your* new employer and HR role. Don't just copy Jill's or anyone else's. A generic plan defeats the purpose of the exercise.

3. **In developing your plan, focus on the "what," not the "how."** That is, scope out the broad targets you'll focus on. There's no need to provide detailed specifics on implementing each task because you'll need to figure those out later.

4. **Use the rest of the rules in this book** to identify specific action items to include in your plan.

Bottom line, you need a roadmap to accelerate your onboarding no matter where you get your information, no matter what period it covers. It doesn't have to be final or pitch-perfect because you'll want to make changes as items get checked off. But put a starter plan in place even if you have to change it a hundred times.

Treat your plan as a **living document** and **conversation tool**. It will evolve and change. You'll want to edit and alter it based on conversations with your manager and emerging issues you unearth after starting.

Let me reiterate: **the key is to work through the items in your onboarding plan <u>while</u> you are fighting fires and doing your job.** Neglecting your onboarding and successful integration into the organization will bite you in the butt down the road. So, put time on your calendar to <u>do both.</u>

'Nuff said.

Summary & Action Steps

Take charge by **developing a one-page Onboarding Plan.** The key steps include:

1. Getting input from your boss, key influencers, and predecessor.
2. Utilizing the Jill Navarro model as one example.
3. Focusing more on the "what" than the "how."
4. Cherry-picking action items from the rest of the Rules in this book.

Revise it regularly as you successfully execute items on your list.

Use your plan to help you maintain your **focus on your major onboarding priorities** and minimize the inevitable day-to-day fires and distractions.

* * *

New HR Leader
Best Practice Tool 2.1:

EXAMPLE 100 DAY
ONBOARDING PLAN

You can also download a copy of this example as a word
doc at → **http://SuccessInHR.com/leader-807191**
(This is in a .zip file. If you have any issues downloading
this file, email me at alan@successinhr.com.)

Jill Navarro
Director - Human Resources
Emerging Technology Division, XYZ Corporation

Overall Goal

At the end of 100 days, I will significantly deepen my knowledge
of the business, essential HR practices, and my business leaders'
priorities. I will also have built positive relationships with all key
influencers.

I will have positively contributed to the organization in clearly
visible ways. I will focus initially on a couple of small, early
wins to increase my credibility and visibility within the division.

And then, I will assume the leadership in launching two major
initiatives -- the ABC critical talent retention project and XYZ
employee productivity initiative working with the corporate HQ
group.

First 30 Days
(Meet/Learn/Understand)

Key Priorities:
- Meet with my manager, John Washington, VP - Talent &
  Organization Development, to clarify our department's
  specific short- and long-term goals. Pinpoint specific vi-
  tal objectives I must deliver over the first 30-100 days.
  Identify a buddy/mentor.

- Finalize my list of key people (influencers) within the Emerging Technology division. Complete informal coffee chats, meet and greets, lunches or meetups with all of them. This includes team members, clients, business leaders, colleagues and management. Identify key issues, past successes, important relationships, and assess company culture.
- Hold the first meeting with my team. Use it to understand existing team priorities, issues, and potential opportunities. Start individual one-on-one update sessions. Re-set performance expectations and start one-on-one bi-weekly updates.
- Pinpoint and understand the most important needs and priorities of my key clients (the six business leaders, two technology leaders, and their teams).
- Identify who else within the company (outside of my division) I should meet with. Ask John Washington for a list of the 10 key people outside of the department that I should get to know, and then set up meet and greets with those people.
- Clarify any external relationships that I need to build (i.e., search firms, consultants, or vendors?). Reach out to make initial contacts where needed. Understand the existing relationships and the nature of any current contracts or commitments that may have been made.
- Complete the company onboarding program, training, and/or self-learning process to get up to speed on products, services, policies, procedures, and company culture.
- Determine if there are any learning gaps I need to address? (i.e., training on the new HR intranet platform, key HR metrics, the performance management system, employee handbook, daily newsletter, etc.)?

Day 31-60
(Strategize/Plan)

Key Priorities:
- Ensure all my plans for the first 30 days are completed.

- Meet with my manager, John W., to gather personal feedback and assess progress in the first 30 days. Determine any new priorities and adjustments needed for the next 30-60 days.
- Determine if any performance problems exist or if terminations may be needed within my direct report team. Begin the process of confidentially discussing severance packages, exit timings, and restructuring options. Engage John W., the Legal group, and others as needed.
- Continue to have bi-weekly one-on-one update meetings with my direct report team to assess their progress and to provide feedback.
- Gather feedback from my key clients. Confirm their priorities and any adjustments needed for the next 30-60 days. Work through any conflicts with them or my manager.
- Take the initiative on the changes to the ABC leadership development project and the XYZ employee incentive program. These 2 key projects represent "early wins" and will help establish me in a positive way within the organization.
- Begin to strategize on a major HR initiative to focus on in the final 40-day period of the 30-60-100-Day plan. This is a "breakthrough" or potentially "game-changing" initiative.

Days 61-100
(Execute/Overdeliver)
Key Priorities:
- Meet with John W. and my key clients to assess the first 60 days and develop a plan for the next 40 days and the rest of the first year.
- Exceed monthly talent/engagement metrics in the key businesses I'm supporting. Assess where we stand against our "company of choice" imperative with the key talent we want to attract and retain. Identify any roadblocks.

- Continue to network with successful HR directors/HR VPs throughout the organization in other divisions to identify best practices in areas essential for success in the businesses I support (e.g. staffing, retention, engagement, emerging strategic initiatives, etc.) Set up monthly conference calls to share ideas in these areas.
- Execute and follow through on actions related to the changes to the ABC key talent retention project and the XYZ employee productivity initiative. Gather feedback on how these 2 "early win" projects are going and make any adjustments where needed.
- Create a pilot program for [*specific new HR "breakthrough" initiative*] and implement it on a small-scale basis. Gather team and client feedback. Assess the potential for a full-scale roll-out.
- Develop a one-year plan (and metrics) to dramatically improve retention of E-commerce key talent and improve our reputation in the marketplace for such talent.

*   *   *

Rule #3:
KNOW THE BUSINESS COLD
& HOW YOUR HR ROLE FITS

To paraphrase Pam Fox Rollin, author of _42 Rules For Your New Leadership Role..._

> _As a new [HR] leader, you can be wrong._
> _You can be misinformed._
> _You can be too pessimistic._
> _You can be too optimistic._
> **_But you cannot be clueless_**
> **_about the business._**

In fact, I'd take Pam's point a step further...

> **It's easy to impress your boss, clients and colleagues as the new HR leader,** _when you've impressed them with your knowledge of their business _first.__

Here's the deal. As a new HR leader, you've been hired to be a business partner who will contribute to the success of the business. Yes, I know this is cliché and what everyone in HR says.

However, if you want to gain REAL credibility as a true business/HR leader, from day one, you must craft a **strategic point of view** about the organization you're joining and how your role fits.

So let's talk about how to make that happen.

Let's say, for example, you're just starting at PepsiCo. It's not enough to know that they "sell soda pop and snack food products." Everybody knows that. Instead, if you want to stand out from day one as a business/HR leader, you need to be able to go well beyond this simple sound bite and be able to...

Summarize the Company's Business

So let's do some homework. For your new organization, sit down right now and jot down your thoughts about the following:

- **Products (or Services):** What is the specific array of products (or services) that the organization creates? How do they fit with each other?
- **Competitors:** Who are the top 1-2 main competitors? How does your employer differentiate itself from them?
- **Customers/Market:** What are the target customers of the organization?
- **Making Money:** How does the employer generate revenue and make money?
- **Love and Hate:** How do customers feel about the employer's product or service? What do they love or hate? What are the most common complaints and issues?
- **Metrics:** What are the employer's 2-3 key metrics of success? Which of these business numbers they're doing well on, and which ones they're struggling with?
- **Organization:** How big is the organization? How is it organized? Does everyone report to the CEO, or is it separated into divisions that operate as separate businesses?
- **News and Rumors:** Have there been any interesting news reports about the employer? What is the organization rumored to do? Don't just read these items. Formulate an opinion about them.

Now let's take this a step further...

Summarize the Business Strategy

Why? Because you should know not only *what* products or services the organization provides, but *why* they do so. Knowing the "why" will help you better understand your new employer's view of the world, and you'll come across like a veteran of the company.

For example, if your new employer cares about "providing technology that makes people's lives easier and better" (Apple), then you need to know that. Or if the employer is passionate about "relieving hunger across the nation" (Feeding America), you should be able to talk enthusiastically about that mission.

With this in mind, let's continue the homework. For your organization, jot down your thoughts about the following associated with knowing the business strategy:

- **Mission:** Look up the employer's mission statement. How does it live up to this mission?
- **Strategy:** What is the employer's business strategy? How is it currently executing against it?
- **Values:** What does the employer value? "Values" pertain to anything that's important to them, explicitly or implicitly. To understand this, read interviews with the founders and think about their culture and products. For example, values might include aspects such as "moving fast" (Facebook) or "don't be evil" (Google).
- **Strengths:** Consider the organization's products or services -- what are their most vital selling points? How does the company leverage those? What about the company or its products has enabled its success?
- **Weaknesses:** What are the significant issues, problems, and complaints with the organization and its products (or services)? How does it address those weaknesses?
- **Challenges:** What are the biggest challenges for the organization right now? How are they addressing them? What challenges have they recently overcome?

- **Opportunities:** Is there anything on the horizon (with technology or within their industry) they are capitalizing on?
- **Threats:** Is there anything on the horizon threatening the organization's success?
- **Future:** What do you think the future holds for this employer? Think about any new products or features that would be a natural fit.

Now let's switch up and talk about your role. Think about the HR function or team you'll be leading and...

Summarize Your HR Charter

You know the drill by now. Jot down your thoughts about the following associated with the HR function and team you'll be leading:

- **Business Strategy Linkage:** What is the main problem you've been hired to solve? What HR projects, goals, and key initiatives are you expected to lead that will enable the company to achieve its current business strategy?
- **Team Linkage:** What does your function or team deliver that enables the company to achieve its current strategy? Where does your team fit into the big picture?
- **Leadership Requirements:** How can you thrive as an HR leader in this company? What are strengths you can leverage or capitalize on? What competency or experience gaps will you need to close?
- **Team Requirements:** What must your team be great at to deliver high value? Do you have the horsepower (people, budget) needed to get it done?
- **Connect the dots:** Begin connecting the business and the HR sides of the organization. For example, let's say you're starting at Amazon. They have a reputation for being a low-margin, frugal, and metrics-driven business. Questions you should ask yourself include: *How does this*

affect their HR strategy? Does this mean that all their HR programs and initiatives must be grounded in metrics and done on the cheap? These are the preliminary hypotheses you want to draw from your homework before you arrive.

Now draft a 2-page summary that captures the essence of these three previous Summaries – i.e. The Company's Business, Business Strategy and HR Charter. This is your <u>Strategic Focus.</u>

Don't worry about perfecting this on your first pass. Just get this started early so you can complete it as soon as possible. Having this enables you to start mentally with a solid business and strategic foundation you can build on to become even smarter. If you're already working at the company, this is valuable for you to have as well.

Your goal in going through this exercise is to internalize this information so that you become as familiar with the business as any current leader or insider would. If you don't have enough data or insight to answer these questions, you're not ready to excel in your new job. So, take the time to research, learn and think about these areas.

All of this may sound impossible, but it isn't. There are a variety of steps you can take to facilitate this process.

1. Gather readily available information.

Hit the company website. Go through their annual reports, mission statements, About Us pages, blog, SEC filings, newspaper articles, corporate online videos, support pages, and whatever else pops up on their site.

2. Tap your key influencers.

Ask questions and get perspectives on these strategic summary questions from your boss and key influencers (see Rule #1).

Talk to your predecessor and others you know who have previously worked with the organization. Share your thinking, if appropriate, framed as "I've been wondering how X in the business is affecting Y in HR." Then follow up by asking: "What are your thoughts?"

3. Request key insider data about the organization.

If you haven't joined the organization yet, ask for limited access to the company intranet and corporate web pages to access critical insider data about the business. This could include:

- A password with instructions on how to access the employee intranet.
- Access to more information about HR policies, strategies, or updates about the division or business unit you are joining. This includes the mission, goals, and objectives.
- Organization charts and forms.
- The phone directory or a list of key contacts.

Yes, I know that some of this is *confidential* (and therefore unavailable) until you officially set foot on the premises. *But request it anyway.* The best organizations are not hesitant to share this information with their top talent, especially once you've signed on to the organization.

You want to get as much info as you can beforehand to enable you to spend your valuable first days on more productive activities.

4. Use the product or service.

No matter what HR role you're moving into, you should attempt to use the product or service if you haven't already.

Clearly, this isn't always practical. It's easy if it's a consumer product like clothing, computers, or food – or a service like banking. However, it's tougher if they make and sell equipment for astronauts. But do it if you can, as it will help you answer the question: "Have you ever used our product (or service)?"

Keep in mind your goal as a new HR leader will be to create value and serve clients who work directly on the product or service. And being a user or consumer yourself is the first step in understanding their issues.

Summary & Action Steps

Develop your own two-page Strategic Focus. It requires in-depth organizational homework but is indispensable to your success as a new HR leader.

It should capture:

- The organization's business
- The organization's strategy
- Your HR charter (and how it aligns with the business)

Internalizing this document will enable you to make a powerful impression on your boss, clients, and colleagues in conversations.

Once you have it, update it monthly as you learn more and the business situation and your role evolve. It's one of the most essential tools in your HR leadership toolbox. So, don't let it get stale.

* * *

Rule #4:
STEP UP & TAKE CHARGE WITH CONFIDENCE ON DAY ONE

Starting on day one, the best HR leaders begin working towards building trust and credibility.

So should you.

To make this happen, here is a list of **eight trust and credibility-building priorities** you should undertake:

Priority #1
Don't Get Blindsided
On Your First Day.

This is especially crucial if you're being hired from the outside. As mentioned, when you arrive on day one, many people will no doubt be waiting to consume your time.

However, your most important day-one priority should be to <u>meet with your boss first</u>, preferably as early in the morning as possible. The purpose of doing this is NOT to score points, brown-nose, or have them hold your hand.

The real reason for this crucial day-one meeting was summed up well by my former boss, Jim McConnaughay. Jim served in various HR VP roles at Fisher Price Toys, Golden Grain Foods, and Quaker Oats.

Here is Jim's take:

Your worst nightmare as a new HR leader is to show up on your first day – not knowing, for example, that rumors of mas-

sive management layoffs are circulating...or that a major re-organization...or merger...or union organizing drive...or new CEO may be announced later that week.

Any of these situations will be significant distractions to your team, clients, and the entire organization – and will impact your ability to get off to a fast start.

And yes, they all have happened to ME!

That's why, according to Jim, this day-one boss meeting is essential. Even if it lasts only 20 minutes, it will keep you from being surprised, blindsided, and operating under old assumptions that may have changed since you said "yes" to the offer.

You should have this meeting even if you're an insider promoted into your new role. Why? Because you may now be privy to Board-classified or confidential information you might not have been ever eligible to know about before.

Ideally, here's your strategy for this day-one meeting with your boss:

- Get insight into recent organizational changes, emerging issues with your new team, and any watch-outs since you accepted the offer. *Ideally, you want to gather this information in real-time, where you can look your boss in the eye, read their non-verbals and follow up with probing questions accordingly.*

- Get advice on the most urgent issues that you'll need to address. Also, get some initial reactions to your draft Onboarding Plan (Rule #2). You'll also want to know if any job accountabilities have changed since the interview or your last discussion. Also, dig into what's keeping the boss up at night.

- At the very minimum, you'll want to walk away knowing your 2-3 key priorities for the first 30 days, your boss' preferred way of communicating, how you should provide updates, and how frequently.

Bosses travel. Attend meetings all day. Have their own agendas to drive. And some have been known to be unavailable for their new people on day one.

That's why you should block time on your new boss' calendar as soon as you accept the offer – and strongly request that this be a **"no-cancel" meeting.** It will help you avoid a potentially awkward and unproductive start.

In fact, you should connect on day one with your boss **before meeting with anyone else...especially before your first official meeting with your staff,** for all the reasons previously mentioned.

Priority #2:
Hold A Very Brief "Get Acquainted" Staff Meeting.

With the meeting with your boss out of the way, the meeting with your staff becomes your next priority.

If you CAN accomplish this on your first day, that's ideal. If not, come in on day one and schedule it for your second or third day.

Don't put this off.

Your new direct reports will be understandably curious and concerned about what the new boss is like, so don't keep them waiting and wondering. Being "missing in action" is not a great way to hit the ground running. Again, first impressions matter.

Even if you've met them all individually beforehand, pull the group together anyway. Many will have already googled you, looked up your profile on LinkedIn, and developed initial impressions – good and bad. So, take charge of the team immediately and begin crafting your narrative.

Here's what you'll want to cover in this *extremely short* group meeting:

- Express your enthusiasm and optimism about joining the team.
- Share a little background information about yourself.

- Discuss your overall style of operating.
- Share initial and broad expectations you have of your staff.
- If appropriate, have your staff members to introduce themselves as well.
- **Indicate you'll be setting up one-on-ones in the next few days.**
- If some of your direct reports are in remote locations, zoom or conference call them into the meeting.

That's it. Focus only on intros, icebreaking, and connecting. Nothing in-depth like the strategic HR plan or critical priorities for the next year ...it's too early for all that.

It's better for this meeting to be too short than too long. This is **foundational.** You'll have plenty of opportunities to build on this initial contact with the team.

Here's a <u>second option</u>:

This option is most relevant if you've been promoted from within or already know the team. If this is the case, you might choose to do a *New Manager Assimilation Meeting* within your first week.

You can find a template for doing one of these sessions at the end of this chapter as *New HR Leader Best Practice Tool 4.1.*

A *New Manager Assimilation Meeting* can significantly speed up your onboarding time – and it provides these other benefits:

- It gets all the questions that your people really want to ask on the table early.
- It does this in a forum where everyone can simultaneously hear what you have to say.
- It can kill early rumors and misunderstandings and go a long way toward building trust.

This requires more time to set up and prepare for – which is why it can't happen immediately.

But taking a few extra days to get it right is worth it.

Again, check out the process and the requirements for making this type of meeting work for you at the end of this chapter.

Priority #3:
Don't Overreact To The Staff's
Initial Responses To You.

Your team members are dealing with their own issues about having a new boss. Some may complain to your face. Some will stroke your ego. And still others will avoid you or bury their real feelings entirely.

Don't mistake these reactions to your arrival for competence at their jobs or openness to embracing your new way of doing things. On the contrary, your loudest initial dissenter may well become your strongest ally.

Experience has shown that your brightest, most savvy team members are among those most likely to push back on your decisions, frustrate you initially, and leave prematurely if treated with anything less than authenticity, candor, and respect. So give everyone a little breathing room at the beginning to adapt to the new sheriff in town.

Priority #4:
Get a Baseline Assessment
Of Your New Team.

Talk to your boss or your **predecessor** (if available) about each of your direct report's past performances. Get copies of performance reviews, 360 assessments, special recognition awards, or other documents that speak to their current performance and future potential.

When you start meeting with your clients, use this as an opportunity to validate any early assessments you have about individual members of your team as well.

You want to determine:
- Who is capable and who is not?
- Who can be trusted and who can't?
- Who has influence and why?

Objectivity here is important.

In the short run, knowing their skills and competencies will guide you as you begin to assign projects, tasks, and key initiatives.

In the long run, it's crucial to understand who **your top performers are, who you can go into battle with, and who may need to be cut from the team (see Rule #11).** Therefore, probe for examples of performance so that you aren't biased by perceptions unsupported by evidence.

Priority #5:
Schedule One-on-Ones.

These should start by your first or second week, and these initial individual meetings may continue for a couple of weeks, depending on how many direct reports you have. **Even if you know you will be reorganizing or potentially terminating some people go at a later date, make it a point to talk to each team member.** Give everyone their day in court.

Your goal is to go out of your way to sit down with everyone on your team face-to-face to learn more about them, relying upon the following five questions as an agenda:

1. What's the story and history of this team?
2. What's going well in your position and with our team?
3. What's not working? What do we need to do more or less of that would make our team even stronger or your contributions to the department even more valuable?
4. What are your expectations of me as your manager?
5. What can I do to help you be successful?

Don't hesitate to probe even deeper beyond these initial questions. Many new HR leaders will use their first one-on-ones as a way to establish their authority and set priorities. And that's fine.

But this is also actually your best (and sometimes only) chance to learn about these people as people. What motivates them? What are their aspirations? What do they need to succeed? What kind of person are they at work? What kind of work environment will make them thrive? This is an incredible chance to connect with your team members and establish areas of commonality.

Listen and take good notes during these sessions. **Seize upon any easy issues to fix. However, resist the temptation to make promises you can't keep.** Personal promises of raises, promotions, or juicy work assignments made by your predecessor should not be honored until you've had a chance to check them out first and consider whether they still make sense in the new world under your leadership.

Finally, once you've had a chance to digest the comments from these meetings and combine them with your own thinking, consider distributing a summary to the team. Such a note will clarify some of your initial expectations and cover such areas as:

- Current team strengths, issues, and opportunities facing our team.
- How we'll maintain ongoing communication with the team.
- Key goals, outcomes, and priorities going forward.

This summary note represents your "top-line impressions" and should not reveal names. The value of debriefing the overall outcomes from your meetings with the broader team is to **validate the current state of the team** and **provide some initial direction** under your leadership.

When you clarify expectations upfront in this way, it helps build trust with your new team and eliminates negative surprises and disappointments.

Priority #6:
Soothe Ruffled Feathers.

If you have been promoted to manage people who were once your peers, some may be jealous or considered themselves candidates for your job. Some may even work to undermine you. This may subside with time.

But expect some early tests of your authority.

When this happens, address them, especially if these individuals are your top performers or high-potentials. When you know by their actions and comments that they are hurt and unhappy, don't wait. Choose the right moment to speak to them directly but supportively, offering something along the lines of:

> *Bill, I know you're likely disappointed you didn't get the job. Candidly, I know I would be. But I want you to know I'm aware of your significant contributions to this team, and I will ask for your input and ideas as we make decisions moving forward. I value your opinion a lot and want to ensure I provide you with all the support you need to succeed.*

And then, *by your actions*, give the relationship time to work. Many may come around to acceptance and support. Obviously, if some cannot adjust to you as their new boss and choose to start undercutting you, then you should take stronger action, including removing them from the team (see *Rule #11*).

Don't make the mistake of expecting your boss to soothe bruised egos and resentments before you arrive. My experience is that this isn't sufficient to address the pain and disappointment some may feel by not being promoted to your job. And their resentment may still reside below the surface for some time unless you acknowledge or address this personally.

So step up to the plate. Getting others to accept you as the leader is an essential part of your role. Ignoring them tells these team members you lack the confidence to deal with difficult situations.

Priority #7:
Respect the Past.

Take time to learn about the past. Don't just make changes for the sake of change. Don't just put your fingerprints on things to let everyone know you are there and because you are the boss. It makes you look foolish, insensitive, and arrogant.

Below is an example of what happens when this advice isn't followed. This was conveyed to me recently by a personal friend, a VP of HR, about one of his former direct reports.

I'll tell you the real story. Rick fell flat on his face when I hired him as the HR manager in our Financial Services division – primarily because he disrespected his new team.

I gave him the mandate to "develop and take his new HR team to the next level." **But in the process, he refused to value and acknowledge the great relationships his team had already established with their clients. He also arrogantly discounted their great performance results, which weren't done on his watch.**

As a result, he never won them over.

And when his best two direct reports resigned in frustration for "better opportunities," it got even worse. He told the remaining team members to pick up the slack while continuing to deny them the much-needed praise and recognition they were hungry for.

His insensitive, tone-deaf actions caused the team's morale and performance to drop further. With no other choice, I fired Rick's butt after his first annual review.

The point: don't disrespect the past successes of your team and those who have contributed to them. However, as you're giving respect, you deserve to receive it as well, which brings us to…

Priority #8:
Never Apologize For Your Selection As The Leader.

This is more of a mindset to adopt rather than an action step to take, but it is important nevertheless. It was described well by Mike Feiner, a former senior HR executive at PepsiCo, in his great book, *The Feiner Points of Leadership.* Mike learned this important lesson when his boss asked him to lead an HR task force earlier in his career when he was Director of Organization Planning. Here's Mike's candid account of this situation:

I was a bit surprised that I was asked to head up the task force. I was twenty-nine at the time, and most of the field labor relations people were ten to fifteen years older than me. But I was psyched. And this would be great for my visibility.

I decided I needed to call a meeting of all the field HR executives. These six executives reported to my boss and would be responsible for implementing the strategy we would be developing for the Teamsters. I'd be the one who'd lead the team in crafting the strategy. So naturally, I told my boss that I was scheduling the meeting, and he was fine with it.

Being ever so clever, I thought it would make sense prior to the meeting to have a conference call with the six field veterans. I figured they might be a bit annoyed that Hot Shot Mike was put in charge, even though we were all technically at the same level in the organization. I felt a conference call would be the best way to announce this all-day working session I was going to convene.

The conference call was brief: It didn't need to be a song and dance.

"Listen, folks, I appreciate your taking a few minutes. This won't take more than that. I'm not quite sure why Ed asked me to head up this thing – you all have a lot more seasoning than I do – but this Teamster deal is one we need to get our arms around."

I paused, waiting for any reactions. Silence on the line.

"Would you look at your schedules? I'd like to get going on this. How about next Tuesday here in New York? We can spend the whole day framing our strategy for beating these guys. Will that work for everybody?"

To my surprise, no one voiced a problem with the meeting date. "I'll see you guys next Tuesday morning," was my close. The call had taken less than five minutes. Naturally, I followed up with a confirming memo.

Tuesday rolled around and I was ready. However, by 8:30AM, no one had arrived and I was beginning to get the sense that I'd be meeting with myself.

Finally, I made a call to Jack, based in Kansas City, a grizzled and gruff veteran of union wars who had taken a liking to me despite my youth (and MBA).

My heart sank when Jack answered his phone.

"Jack, it's Mike. How come you're not coming to our meeting?"

He paused. "You want the truth or should I tell you the line, you'll hear from the other guys, like we got a slowdown or they're sabotaging the baggage carts or some crap like that?"

"The truth would work, Jack."

"Well, most of us lost respect for you last week. You called and told us about the meeting, then apologized for being in charge. Remember?"

"Jack, I was just trying to be sensitive to you guys. I mean, you're probably not happy that Ed gave me this assignment. I was just trying to be sensitive."

"Listen, son, we weren't too thrilled either that Ed's fairhaired boy was leading this team. 'Cause you don't know shit about this stuff even though you're smart. And 'cause it makes us feel older than we want to admit, you being in your twenties. But in apologizing to us, you were kinda puttin' us on. And you demeaned yourself."

I was stunned – but I understood instantly what Jack was saying. **Being angry with Ed for putting me in charge was their problem. Apologizing for it made it my problem.** *They sensed immediately that my apology was given not because I regretted being in charge, but because I wanted to appear overly sensitive to their concerns, and they'd seen straight through me and didn't believe I was being authentic.*

I'm not suggesting you should strut your stuff and act like a pompous jerk when you're put in charge. But there's no percentage in rubbing people's noses in your new leadership role, no matter how happy you might be at being

appointed. Apologizing for your leadership appointment damages your credibility, and signals a lack of commitment to the team. And high-performance leaders don't do it.

And new HR leaders shouldn't do it either. Mike Feiner's counsel is wise on this point. If you've worked hard and earned your title, you can be grateful and humble – but you have absolutely nothing to apologize for. So, don't.

Summary & Action Steps

Chances are the team had a leader before you. They may have adored that leader and they may love the work they do. There may be a real fear that you, as the new boss, will come in and turn everything upside down.

Don't! At least, not before allowing yourself sufficient time to get to know your staff and their history. Also, make these **eight items** part of your game plan:

1. Meet your boss on day one to avoid surprises.
2. Hold a very brief "Get Acquainted" staff meeting. Consider holding a New Manager Assimilation Meeting if you already know the team.
3. Don't overreact to your staff's initial responses to you.
4. Get a baseline assessment of your new team.
5. Schedule one-on-ones.
6. Soothe ruffled feathers.
7. Respect the past.
8. Never apologize for your selection as the leader.

These steps will do wonders for your credibility and ability to build trust with the team. Once armed with more complete knowledge of your staff, you can begin taking further actions to enhance their performance.

* * *

New HR Leader
Best Practice Tool 4.1:
THE NEW MANAGER
ASSIMILATION MEETING

You can also download a copy of this tool as a word
doc at → **http://SuccessInHR.com/leader-807191**
(This is in a .zip file. If you have any issues downloading
this file, email me at alan@successinhr.com.)

The New Manager Assimilation Meeting is designed to dramatically speed up your onboarding time.

It does this by getting all your team's *real* and *hidden* questions on the table early on in a forum where everyone can hear what you have to say at the same time. All of this goes a long way toward building trust.

This does take time to prepare for, which is why it can't happen immediately. But taking a few additional days to plan and set up this type of meeting up is worth it. Because it gets everyone on the same page quickly. It prevents Jill from filtering the message to Jamal, who filters it again to Jane and so on. Of course, there will always be rumors.

But this process, first popularized by GE over thirty years ago, goes a long way to squelching most of the scuttlebutt early.

Another option: If you decide to utilize this tool, you might also want to consider reaching out to an internal OD specialist or neutral third party to facilitate this meeting. It's not mandatory but does have advantages.

They can help you manage the meeting process, better probe and draw out of the team their questions and concerns…all of which they might be hesitant about sharing in front of you, their new boss. You don't want to use a process designed to increase trust to inadvertently quash it.

How to conduct this meeting

1. **When you first come aboard, convene a meeting with your team members during your first week.** While in the room, mention the objectives for the meeting, give all team members a chance to introduce themselves, and say a little about who they are and what they do.

2. **Then, leave the room.** While you're *out* of the room, have the team answer these questions:
   a. What do we expect of our new leader?
   b. What do we want the new leader to know about us? What do we do well? Where do we need improvement?
   c. What do we want to know about the new leader? What are our concerns about him or her?
   d. What are the burning issues in our department?
   e. What are the major obstacles the new leader will face?

3. **Have all answers posted on a flip chart.** But make sure they're anonymous so that you (the leader) won't later be able to connect the comments to any one specific team member.

4. **After a break, reconvene with your team and go over the responses that have been posted on the flip chart.** Feel free to ask questions about what has been posted and explore the ways in which you can take quick action on some of the answers.

5. **Conclude the meeting** by ending on a positive note, thanking everyone for their participation and reiterating any next steps you plan to take.

6. **Distribute a summary** to the team of key points made and next steps you plan to take.

How to best prepare for this meeting

1. **Send out an agenda** to the team ahead of time to let them know exactly what to expect.

2. **Line up a third-party facilitator**, should you decide to use one.

3. **Then prepare yourself** by not going in cold. Instead, think ahead of time about what you want to tell your team about yourself – both personally and professionally.

    Use the points below to help you prepare. Also, consider what examples, stories, or anecdotes you might want to share that illustrate your points.

    About you
    *   Family, Personal Background
    *   Hobbies, Interests
    *   HR/Professional background/Philosophy
    *   Education / Experience

    Leadership Biases
    *   What are your leadership strengths? Weaknesses?
    *   What qualities do you believe are essential for a top performer in HR to possess?
    *   How do you deliver feedback (both positive and negative)?
    *   How will your team find how you feel about their performance?
    *   What drives you to do your best?
    *   How do you motivate others to do their best?

    Decision making
    *   How do you go about making decisions?
    *   What types of decisions do you see as directive, consultative or consensus?

Communication

- In what way and how often do you like others to communicate with you?
- How much detail do you prefer to have?
- Under what circumstances do you feel that you must be in the loop?
- And under what circumstances is being in the loop not as important to you?

Conflict resolution

- What are your "hot" buttons?
- If your team upsets or disappoints you, how will the members know?
- How do you like conflict to be resolved?
- What is the best way to give you feedback?

Benefits of this meeting

This effort can speed up discovering unspoken concerns, misunderstandings, and disconnects. **In addition, the anonymity of this exercise can bring to the surface more issues in one day than weeks of one-on-one meetings.**

Dirty laundry can be aired along with the natural anxieties that arise when a new, yet familiar boss comes in. And in this open atmosphere, questions can be surfaced in a safe environment.

When done successfully, it clears the decks enabling you to better drive your agenda for the first few months.

*　*　*

Rule #5:
GET ON TOP OF KEY
PROJECTS & DON'T LET GO

Once you've broken the ice with your team, **schedule an early meeting within your first ten days with the entire team to get a full review of all open projects, initiatives, and HR deliverables.**

Ask them to come prepared with a spreadsheet listing the projects they're working on. These should be laid out as follows:

- Brief description of the project
- Client to whom the project relates
- Current status (% completed or target date for completion)
- Obstacles (if any) to the successful completion.
- A "confidence rating" that the deadline or deliverable will be met. *To keep this simple, use the old tried-and-true "red-yellow-green" system.* That is, use some kind of red, yellow, or green symbol (an "X," or a checkmark, for example) to indicate the level of confidence that the deadline or deliverable will be achieved – e.g., **green** (highly confident), **yellow** (cautiously optimistic, minor issues), or **red** (major concerns, problems or obstacles).

To further clarify what you want, develop and provide a **simple spreadsheet template** (with the above bullets as column headers) to everyone in advance. Also, give an **example** of a couple of filled-in projects to illustrate. This will further clarify what you want, standardize what everyone provides, and allow you to digest the information quickly.

Ideally, you'll leave this meeting with a consolidated list of everything your team is currently accountable for. You'll also better grasp your team's workload and pressing issues.

As a result of this first project/key deliverables review meeting, you may need to immediately personally intervene in some cases to get projects back on track or to communicate a change in the timeline to a client or your boss. But it's better to be proactive in your early weeks rather than let it derail you further down the line.

This is a valuable early meeting, even if you were promoted from within this team. You may be familiar with the projects on the table, but it's unlikely that you've had all the details of each project. And assuming you know where things stand without verifying your facts is risky. It's far better to approach your team's work as if it were entirely new to you rather than gloss over details and miss some crucial points.

Summary & Action Steps

Compile a spreadsheet outlining the critical priorities of your team and maintain it.

Utilize it as a powerful <u>management tool</u> and keep it current by having your team members update it monthly. You can then meet with them individually or collectively for status updates.

This will allow you to stay on top of new and completed projects and key initiatives in the future.

* * *

Rule #6:
SUCCESSFULLY MANAGE YOUR SINGLE MOST IMPORTANT WORKING RELATIONSHIP

"You don't have to like or admire your boss, nor do you have to hate him. **However, you DO have to manage him so that he becomes your resource for personal achievement, accomplishment, and success.**"

Who said this? Peter Drucker, the legendary guru of management, in his book, *The Practice of Management,* way back in 1954 – when practically all bosses were "he's" and "him's."

Even though times have changed dramatically, his advice is true today, especially if you want to succeed in your first 100 days as a new HR leader.

There is no other working relationship that is more important. Your boss has the keys to unlock doors that will remain closed if you fail to nurture this relationship. They are the one who plays a critical role in connecting you to the essential influencers throughout the organization you need to know in your early days. They can lobby on your behalf for more resources to deliver your HR initiatives. They can assign you to projects that can give you much-needed early "wins" to help you establish yourself. And, of course, you won't progress, get rewarded, or even stay employed without your boss' strong support.

Obviously, none of this is breaking news.

However, making this all happen is easier said than done. The problem is that no two bosses are alike. They come in all flavors and varieties; unfortunately, you don't get to choose your preference. Too often, we work for people who are difficult, tough to "decode," or smart but inaccessible. To illustrate this latter point...

Let Me Tell You About One Boss
I Had At Quaker Oats Who Was Brilliant
But Tough To Get To Know.

He was extremely introverted. Now, there's nothing wrong with introverts. Some of the world's best leaders, such as Elon Musk, Tim Cook, and Warren Buffet, fall into this category. I'm an introvert myself. And in my boss' case, he knew the business cold. He was a highly respected HR senior executive that had progressed rapidly in the organization because he was off-the-charts brilliant.

But he was also extremely withdrawn, standoffish, and didn't open up to many people. He wasn't big on team meetings and lots of personal interaction – preferring email and brief five-minute updates instead.

And when he got pissed off, which was surprisingly often, he said nothing. Instead, he'd indicate his displeasure through his well-known "death stare." Everyone on the team had experienced this terrifying stone-faced frown at least once. And it was worse than getting cussed out.

Consequently, when I first joined his headquarters team as one of his four HR directors, I was advised by my peers to stay out of his way and to keep conversations with him brief and strictly business.

I did that for about a month.

That was when I decided to go against their advice. I determined that having an "arm's length" relationship with this boss was simply asinine.

So, I took a risk.

I invited him to travel with me to investigate some employee relations concerns at a few of my assigned regional locations, not knowing how he would respond.

Since I was a rookie, I figured I'd use the old "new kid on the block" routine as my excuse if he decided to give me his trademark stare.

He didn't.

Instead, he jumped at the chance to join me on the road.

Frankly, I didn't need his help because these were fairly typical HR issues. And I hesitated for a moment, wondering if I really wanted him around looking over my shoulder.

But I'd heard rumors that he'd create any excuse to travel on business to escape the corporate headquarters bubble, where he was clearly uncomfortable. Traveling with me gave him such an excuse.

Things worked out well.

I used that time on airplanes, in hotel lobbies, and in rental cars to break the ice and go to school on him. As he talked about his family, kids, hobbies, education, and previous jobs, our relationship began to slowly transform.

Over time, he taught me a lot about the business, HR...and himself.

I learned more about his operating style.

I learned his in-depth reasoning behind our team goals.

I learned about the subjects he was passionate about.

I learned when he liked starting in the morning.

I learned when he liked to go deep into the details and when he preferred to be hands-off.

For example, he revealed that because he started his career in field operations and still loved it, he wanted to stay heavily involved in employee relations. However, he made it clear that he didn't give a crap about the headquarters OD and team building programs we were working on -- and so he gave me lots of runway on those initiatives.

I discovered how he played corporate politics too. I noted those situations when he didn't hesitate to throw his weight around, using his "death stare" and superior HR smarts with the higher-ups to get what he wanted. I also marveled at his approach in those few instances when he would try to impress them.

I also discovered not to attempt to reach him at 10 AM or 2 PM. At these times, he'd generally duck out to grab a smoke, a habit he had concealed from everyone but his executive assistant.

I used all this information to effectively manage my relationship with him. This meant I did not focus on creating warm and fuzzy interactions because he wasn't that type of guy. Instead, I quietly supported his agenda, took projects off his plate that disinterested him, and did the little noticeable things that made him look good – without promoting myself and being in his face all the time.

In return, he always made time for me on his schedule for coaching, advice, or to share his prodigious intellect. I also got a couple of excellent performance reviews from him too. And it became one of the best HR assignments I've ever had.

But more importantly, this experience taught me that no matter what you initially think of your boss or his style, you have to OWN this relationship.

And that means you must...

Go First. Waiting for Your Boss to Reach Out To You – Creates Success in Waiting, Not In Building the Relationship

Said differently, as a newbie, you must be prepared to take complete charge of growing the relationship with your boss and be prepared to do ALL the heavy lifting. To make this happen, you need to:

1. Drive the **critical conversations** with your boss that will make you successful.

2. Embrace the **basics of effectively managing your boss** – no matter who the boss is or what kind of operating style they have.

Let's talk more about these items, one by one, starting with...

The Six Critical Conversations You Must Drive With Your Boss

In his fantastic book, *The First 90 Days* (a major inspiration for this book), Michael Watkins first discussed the necessity of having separate, meaningful conversations with your boss on specific issues essential to success in your first three months. Most of what I'll share here is based on my experience applying Watkins' ideas, lessons from HR colleagues I've consulted with – and additional insights especially relevant for you as an HR leader.

A few of these talks with your boss should have begun in the interview process before you accepted the job. But if they haven't, they should undoubtedly start immediately after you've joined the organization. And will be built on through constant conversations back and forth over your first 100 days.

That said, here are they are:

Critical Conversation #1: Understand Your Boss' Goals.

You must know your boss's goals, objectives, and major priorities. Everything you do is potentially linked back to these hot buttons and can be used to your benefit when completing your assignments and determining your priorities.

To get your arms around their goals, ask for a copy of their performance objectives or the key HR priorities for their area of the organization.

Then schedule a one-on-one meeting to discuss them – and the rationale for them – in depth. Besides helping you in your work, this shows you care about the bigger picture.

Additionally, you can use this information to anticipate their needs and stay one step ahead of them. For example, if one of their goals is to develop a Global Strategic HR Plan for the organization and an initial meeting is coming up in two weeks, beat them to the punch by asking what you can help them prepare so that the session runs smoothly for them.

Critical Conversation #2:
Determine the Boss' Initial
Expectations of You.

Once you know their goals, you'll want to understand what they need from you immediately (in the first 30 days) and short-term (first 100 days). This can be done as a separate conversation or as part of Conversation #1.

Either way, here are the key areas and questions you'll want to comprise your agenda for this meeting:

Your Immediate Performance Priorities
- What results will you need to deliver right away?
- How do these link to your boss' objectives?
- How will your overall performance be measured? When? Formally? Informally? Annually?

Rationale: It's time to get granular and away from generalities. You want to nail down where to focus your immediate time and attention.

For example, suppose you're being brought in to support the Marketing group, and they're pissed that the People Leadership Program your predecessor promised to help them create is unfinished. In that case, you and your boss may agree that this is one area you'll want to jump on fast.

As agreements like these occur, confirm them in a quick email summary note back to your boss to ensure you both stay on the same page.

Also, if your performance will be ultimately assessed in a formal annual review, you'll want to know that too. This will enable you both to agree on a more complete set of **longer-term** performance goals. However, this is best done in a separate discussion (covered in Rule #8).

Important Early Wins
- What "early wins" (see Rule #14) or significant initiatives do you need to make progress on in the short term?

- How will ultimate success on these be measured?

Rationale: You should place at the top of your priority list progress against those "hot button" major initiatives your boss cares about most. Some you'll be able to complete within the 100-day time frame. Some you won't be able to finish but are expected to make good progress against.

What's Off Limits?

- What parts of the organization does your boss consider proprietary or in the "no-touch" zone? This includes people, locations, clients, HR policies, or talent programs.

Rationale: You don't want to find out too late that your plan to make drastic changes in that flextime program for working moms is a program that your boss developed and is emotionally invested in. Or you plan to replace someone on your team loyal to your boss.

So you need to understand these types of untouchables subtly. But getting this information is tricky. And often, even they won't know what these are until they're threatened. So you'll need to do some detective work, talk to colleagues, and dig into your boss's personal history.

You can also float a proposed change by them as one of those "I've been thinking about" ideas and then closely watch your boss' facial expression and body language.

Critical Conversation #3: Learn the Way Your Boss Prefers To Communicate.

In this area, don't assume anything. Don't assume that what you think is an appropriate way of communicating with your new boss will match their needs and style.

Again, no two bosses are alike. So you need to ask how they prefer to receive your communications and updates. For example, do they prefer a weekly status report (bullets only) or would they rather meet every other week for one-on-ones? By asking this up front, you will avoid wasting time preparing reports they'll never read.

I've had bosses who prefer to keep 90% of all communications with me by e-mail and voicemail rather than in-person – like the boss I previously described.

And I've had other bosses in an entirely different time zone who preferred frequent, almost daily in-person phone calls to stay on top of things.

In these cases, don't take it personally and waste precious time in your first 100 days trying to change them. Instead, adapt.

In general, you should be prepared to utilize the full-range of communications tools at your disposal: one-on-ones, e-mail, phone, voicemail, text, one-page updates or full power point decks, depending on what needs to be conveyed. Your goal is to keep the boss informed on those issues that are essential to them - - and minimize surprises.

Critical Conversation #4:
Secure Needed Resources From Your Boss.

The resources we're referring to here are things such as:
- financial resources
- technology or technical support
- talented people
- political support

Your first step is to ask yourself: "What exactly do I need from my boss to succeed?" The sooner you can clearly answer this question, the faster you can engage in productive discussions with your boss to acquire them.

Many of these conversations will be on-going ones. However, if you can, it's smart to combine all your resource requests and put them on the table simultaneously as soon as possible. Going back to the well every other day with separate tiny, itty-bitty requests will label you as overly needy, high maintenance, and lose credibility.

But major requests are entirely different. In these cases, you may need to be a persistent pest and keep coming back to your boss repeatedly to help reinforce what you need. Some examples:

- *"Boss, to bring in the 100 new software engineers we need in the next 3 months, I will need to supplement my current HR staff with four dedicated external recruiters. This will require **an extra investment** of $200,000 in retainer fees per month..."*
- *"Boss, we're working with Legal to gather the documentation to support the termination of the Finance VP. The morale in his department is horrible, and the evidence is compelling. Since he's the son-in-law of the CEO, this is likely to get very political and embarrassing. I will need your support to bring the CEO on board with our rationale on this to make our decision stick..."*

In these situations, to strengthen your case, you might find it helpful to frame each request as either an **"investment"** or **"support needed"** to help deliver the desired results. Notice how this is done in the previous examples.

Additionally, you should be prepared to back up such major "asks" with as much evidence, hard data, third party observations or analysis as possible.

And then stand firm. You cannot afford to avoid negotiating back and forth with your boss over the most crucial and essential resources you need, no matter how scarce or problematic they may appear at first. Failure in this area can doom your first hundred days.

Critical Conversations #5 & 6

The first four conversations are enough to get you jump-started. Conversations 5 and 6 will typically occur later and consist of:

- **Documenting Your Performance Goals** detailed in Rule #8.
- **Getting Feedback on How You're Doing** detailed in Rule #12.

These two conversations are so important they are covered as separate Rules in this book. This is because they generate various unique yet essential follow-up actions and often consist of a series of diverse conversations. To understand their scope or to get a quick feel for them now, skip ahead to Rules #8 and #12.

To summarize, these are the six critical conversations you must have with your boss. All are important, and a few of them are uncomfortable, but every single one of these six needs to happen, preferably face-to-face.

Let's now build on this foundation by covering…

The Never-Fail Rules for Building A Successful Relationship with Your Boss.

No matter what type of boss you have, there are **seven rules** that will almost never let you down in bonding with your boss and enhancing the relationship. Here they are:

#1: Keep Your Boss' Up To Speed On What You're Doing.

Most bosses hate surprises – obviously. So, keeping your boss up to speed on what you're doing is common sense.

But sometimes updates are requested impromptu. And you'll have to drop everything to brief your boss on an HR project you're working on – because they'll need to update *their* boss on it. You should always be prepared for such unannounced requests.

To cover yourself, have a one-pager ready *at all times* containing key talking points on your major projects. Doing this will score you points for being on top of things and appearing to think well on your feet. Just keep things simple and direct, and you'll maintain control over the conversation.

Afterward, if changes or next steps are discussed, follow up with a short e-mail recap of the conversation as a little electronic paper trail of what went down, just in case.

#2: Flex Your Style.

Early in my career as an HR manager, I had a **dual reporting relationship with two bosses.** Initially, I dealt with these bosses similarly. I stayed on top of critical projects, beat deadlines, and kept them current on what was happening.

But after a few weeks, I realized how differently they responded to me. If I was working on a project for him, the first boss would ask me for an update a couple of weeks before the deadline. The second boss generally forgot that he even made a deadline – he was only interested in knowing when the project was done, so updating him ahead of time on progress was more irritating to him than helpful.

I eventually figured it out. They were two very different people. Although the things I was doing – displaying commitment to each boss's success and owning the outcome of each project – were the same in each case, I began to understand that I needed to change the style in which I did these things to have success with each boss.

The point: No one simple correct style works in all cases. Be prepared to flex your style to connect with your boss and consider how they respond best. Sometimes you may experience tension between varying your style and remaining true to yourself. **The guiding principle here is that you can flex your style but not your values.** You can't be false, artificial, compromise your integrity, or be perceived as a suck-up. Ultimately, you'll lose their respect. Most people, including bosses, respond best to those who are authentic rather than those trying to be someone they aren't.

#3: Bring Solutions, Not Problems.

In sticky situations, it's tempting to lean on your manager for so-lutions and fixes -- not unlike what kids do with their parents. But your boss, like everyone else, is busy as hell putting out their own fires and trying to meet their boss's needs.

So, as an alternative, heed the words of Pamela Hewitt. Pam is my former SVP of Human Resources at PepsiCo, who used to tell our HR team: "I am always available to discuss an organiza-tional issue you're facing. I'll even take you to lunch to talk about it. *But I need you to have 2-3 potential solutions to the problem already thought out before you even attempt to get on my calendar.*"

Following her advice is wise and will position you in your boss's mind as a proactive problem-solver and solution provider, not just a problem identifier. And it will also demonstrate that you have that high-desired "figure-it-out" gene.

#4: When You Screw Up, Fess Up. Fast!

It's going to happen. **We all make mistakes. You will too, no matter how careful you are. And chances are it will happen earlier rather than later in your HR leadership tenure.**

You will say the wrong thing at the right time.

You will misjudge a situation from time to time.

Or you will outright screw things up.

That happened to me as a young HR director working in a small division of my organization. I reported to a fantastic boss who relied heavily on my judgment and experience.

She had taken a risk and promoted me into my first HR direc-tor role primarily because of my relationships and knowledge of the organization.

But the job was a stretch for me and a bit over my head.

She knew it, and I knew it.

But she was willing to take a chance on me.

So, I didn't want to let her down or make her regret her deci-sion.

But in my second month on the job, I had a horrible lapse in common sense and fell short of her expectations.

I screwed up a very complex employee theft investigation and termination case.

My crime was that I didn't involve our legal department and didn't ask all the right questions. And as a result, I didn't gather all the evidence we needed to reach a clear conclusion about the employee…who had been accused of theft twice before.

And my boss went ballistic!

She immediately called me on the carpet and demanded that I explain my error in judgment.

My defenses reared up. My pride and my aggressive instincts all screamed: "Fight! Defend yourself. Think up a good excuse."

Thankfully, in a moment of sanity, I took a more sensible approach. Here's what I said…

"I was wrong. I'm sorry. I know that I still have a lot to learn in this role. Please let me fix it."

Apparently, this reply from a young, cocky HR leader was not what she expected.

I'll never forget the expression on her face: surprise, confusion, acceptance, and something that may have been… admiration.

Whew!

At that moment, I knew I'd done exactly the right thing.

And as a result, she let me push the re-start button, and we immediately involved our legal team.

And together with them, we mapped a detailed strategy to dig deeper into this case. It was arduous work, but they were terrific. And I felt personally embarrassed by my initial attempts to do this all myself -- trying to be the hero.

In any event…

When we finally completed a thorough investigation and presented our evidence to this employee — who had been a complete, utter jerk throughout the entire process — he broke down and confessed to all three thefts.

And we terminated him immediately.

This situation could have destroyed my HR director career before it got off the ground. **Instead, admitting I was wrong helped me earn the trust of my boss. And it taught me that if you mess up, fess up. Fast.**

In these situations, the magic words are:

"I'm sorry."

"I was wrong."

"I made a mistake. I'll get it corrected."

Then take action, resolve the issue -- and THEN GET ON WITH IT!

Honest and humility goes a long way in life and in HR.

#5: Don't Sweat The Credit.

This is very touchy territory.

You need to pick your battles with your boss. And sometimes, you must be okay with letting go of some credit.

For example, it would be terrific if they always told people about your contribution to a specific project.

But that doesn't always happen.

Sometimes it slips the boss' mind to acknowledge or thank you. Sometimes they may fail to remember your early work on that project if they wound up taking it over and running with it.

Or sometimes it's because they are just plain evil and want to get all the glory for themselves and leave you in the dust.

Regardless of the reason, this is a no-win situation, especially if you are new. Because if you raise a fuss, you immediately get labeled as a diva, a liar, or a credit seeker -- none of which helps your image as a team player when trying to establish yourself.

Your best solution in this situation is just to document your results and contributions (see Rule #15), so that a record of your accomplishments can be properly valued and acknowledged at performance review time.

However, if this continues to be an on-going problem beyond your first 100 days, I recommend a sit down with your boss to discuss corrective actions you'd like to see going forward. Obviously, this isn't an easy discussion to have, and you should be prepared with specific examples to make your case, but it'll be even more crucial at that time once you've established yourself in your role.

#6: Cover Your Boss' Blind Spots.

This is at the top of any "make your boss look good" list.

Let's face it: Sometimes, bosses hire you because your strengths compensate for their weaknesses. For example, I tend to be strategic on HR issues but not that detail-oriented.

Because of this blind spot, I've hired HR managers who are great at the microscopic gritty details and terrific at execution and follow-up. They cover my shortcomings well, and they've made me look a lot better than I've had any right to look in many cases. In return, I've promoted many of them into bigger HR jobs because of this fact and because they were great performers.

Ask yourself: Where can I fill in the boss' gaps?

If you're great at preparing presentation documents and your boss isn't, you could help enhance or polish up their PowerPoint decks before critical meetings.

If your strength is HR analytics, metrics, or data analysis, you could provide such insights to your boss so that they might share them with the higher-ups to add further punch to proposals they're recommending.

If your boss has a full plate, offer to move stuff from their plate on to yours. First, however, ensure you're working within your bandwidth and capabilities.

Boss blind spots may not be evident initially and may take time to identify, especially if they aren't forthcoming. However, once you know what they are, helping your boss compensate for them is an opportunity for further collaboration and bonding.

#7: NEVER Disrespect or Contradict Your Boss Publicly.

This is the kiss of death.

If you're looking for a quick one-way ticket to your boss' dog house, this is it. You only need to do it one time. That's right, just one slight slip of the tongue can send your career down in flames faster than you can say "outplacement."

Are you wondering if this is just a scare tactic or if I am trying to tell you something? Well, you should know by now that I'm not above scare tactics. But this time, I am trying to tell you something. And here is that something – keep your trap shut in these situations!

If you're ever in a meeting and your boss is delivering incorrect information, *and his boss is in the room,* DO NOT CORRECT HIM. Even if he's totally wrong. Even if he's going to end up looking like a jerk for being wrong. Even if other people in the room realize he's wrong. Don't do it. Even if he tells you beforehand it's ok to do. Let someone else do the correcting. Let them be the one to "help" the boss.

As you might imagine, there is a story behind all these warnings. And you're right.

One time, at a meeting with the PepsiCo senior leadership team, in response to a question, my boss rambled on and on about our unbelievable progress on diversity and inclusion. He beamed with pride as he, off the top of his head, shared numbers to support our progress in retaining African-American, Latino, and Asian females. Most of us on the team knew that the boss was quoting incorrect numbers. And as I sat back and watched, puzzled glances were being exchanged up and down the table.

My colleagues and I were engaged in a wide-eyed mental telepathy exchange. We were thinking, "Oh my God he's doing it again." But none of us was going to stick our neck out and correct him. His mistake would be realized after the meeting and we'd point this out to him then...not now.

We were all hoping he'd change the subject but he kept going on and on. **Then, the new HR leader who just joined our team, Sharon, chimed in an amiable and helpful tone: "Boss, I think the overall numbers you're referring to are only up 2% over last year, not 22%."**

Well, you could have heard a pin drop in that room.

All eyes turned to the boss. His face turned red and he somehow managed to finesse his way through the rest of the presentation by giving some lame excuse for his error. My well-meaning new colleague looked on with complete fear because she knew immediately that she had screwed up.

After the meeting ended, the boss told Sharon he wanted to see her in his office immediately. We never found out what was said behind those closed doors. And while Sharon didn't get fired, she was very clearly in the boss' doghouse for a long time after that.

Let me be clear: challenging facts and pushing back frequently (even on your boss) is an essential part of being an authentic HR leader. And demonstrating this quality will gain you enormous respect and credibility over time...*but only if you push back and challenge at the right time.* And, doing it an open forum to your boss in front of his boss and other higher ups is <u>not</u> the right time.

If Sharon felt compelled to point out this mistake to the boss, as she should have, a better time would have been to approach him privately after the meeting was over.

Lesson learned. 'Nuff said.

Summary & Action Steps

No single relationship is more important in your first 100 days than the one you forge with your boss.

Success in this area requires driving **six critical conversations** with them, which will enable you to:

1. Understand their goals.
2. Determine their initial expectations of you.
3. Learning the way they prefer to communicate.
4. Secure needed resources for your success.
5. Document your performance goals (Rule #8).
6. Get feedback on how you're doing (Rule #12).

This also requires mastering the **rules and daily behaviors that will help you enhance the relationship**, such as:

1. Keeping your boss up to speed.
2. Flexing your style.
3. Bringing solutions, not problems.
4. When you screw up, fessing up. Fast.
5. Not sweating the credit.
6. Covering your boss' blind spots.
7. Never disrespecting or contradicting your boss publicly.

So take charge. Waiting for the boss to reach out to you first creates success in waiting – not in building the relationship.

* * *

Rule #7:
TURN YOUR CLIENTS INTO RAVING FANS

I once had a very powerful, highly-respected client, a General Manager bluntly, right to my face, tell me this when we first met:

> *I've worked hard to earn <u>MY</u> big title. <u>MY</u> life is really stressful and complicated. As my HR partner, if you can help <u>ME</u> reduce that stress, make <u>MY</u> own life easier or enable <u>ME</u> and my team to get things done quicker, you become immensely valuable to <u>ME</u>. If you can't, stay the hell away and don't bother <u>ME.</u>*
>
> *I don't need you to be the best HR guy on the planet, but I do need to know I can rely on you. If you shoot straight with me, do exactly what you say you're gonna do, consistently and without fail, then you're a damn superstar in my eyes.*
>
> *My wife tells me I have the attention span of a gnat. She's right. So, get to the point when we talk. I don't like HR jargon and psychobabble. Just plain English. Also, if you go too long without contacting me, I'll simply forget you exist. Out of sight, out of mind...that is until I'm in trouble or my team's in trouble. Then I'll wonder, where the hell you've been.*

We wound up getting along great.

Buried beneath all this bluster was a guy with a heart of gold as long as you delivered. When you didn't, there was hell to pay. And frankly, I got my share of butt chewings from him -- all of them deserved!

However, when I did deliver, he was gushing in his praise. He became one of my biggest fans and career advocates, consistently vouching for me to the senior management team and my boss.

It was an extraordinary client experience for me because he made it clear – in no uncertain terms – what mattered to him and what didn't. I never had to guess where he was coming from.

As you know, every client won't be that direct and transparent. With many clients, you'll have to work hard to discover what they *really* want. So, as a newbie, it's up to you to climb into their world, dig out and **address what matters to them most.** That's the key to turning them into fans.

Here are **five strategies** for making that happen:

#1: Do an Early Listening Tour.

Even if you've been in the organization for years, don't assume you already know what your clients want from you and your team. It may be different now that you're at the helm.

Instead, take advantage of being the new kid on the block and go out and validate their needs. An effective way to do this is by setting up initial one-hour meetings with them to ask questions and listen.

To prepare your clients for these discussions, send out the following checklist in advance as your agenda:

1. What's the history of your organization in working with our HR team? (Ask the client to highlight 2-3 accomplishments and 2-3 shortfalls of your group?)
2. What has been our team's overall level of service and responsiveness to your (client) needs? What needs are/aren't getting met? Why?
3. What services/activities have you come to depend on from our team?
4. What are the unique contributions or things we do exceptionally well?
5. What would you like to see changed regarding what you want/need from our team?

6. What services should our team provide to your organization in the future? What do you see as the future role of our team in maximizing your organization's success?
7. What's <u>not</u> the role of our team as you see it?
8. What things should our team start doing? Stop doing? Continue to do? (i.e., Stop-start-continue)
9. If you could wish for anything from our team, what would you wish for? (e.g., No surprises? Helping you retain your top talent?)
10. If we could provide all the things you might wish for, what things would you value most? (Prioritize the wish list).
11. How can I ensure good ongoing communication between your organization and my team? (e.g., How will I find out if it's not going well? Or if everything is okay?)

Asking the "stop-start-and-continue" question (#8) on this checklist is critical. From this ONE straightforward question, you'll get answers back like:

"I'd like quicker turnaround time on compensation decisions. We lost a great Finance Director candidate because you guys were too slow on your end..."

"We need to move faster on developing the leadership development program I discussed with your boss a month ago. Here's why this is so important to our team..."

"I need your HR team to stop distracting my team with time-consuming bureaucracy. For example..."

This is <u>precisely</u> the kind of information you want to get.

These discussions will help your clients crystallize their thinking as they verbalize what they need from you and your team. Encourage them to be brutally candid, and it will better help your team better align with theirs.

#2: Identify the Client Priorities You Will Act On.

From these early listening sessions, let your clients know that you've heard them and share what specific actions you'll be taking based on their comments.

This can take the form of a summary of your findings back to them; or a brief e-mail describing the actions you plan to take. This kind of follow-through will get you and your clients on the same page and create early trust. Also, indicate that going forward, you'd like to continue to get this kind of input and feedback regularly.

This is critical.

Having said all this, prepare to disappoint some people. Develop a reputation (and respect) for being candid and upfront. You won't be able to deliver on everything. And sometimes "no" is the only possible answer. But make sure there's a **good and valid reason.**

For example:

"No, unfortunately, we can't tackle another project this week AND deliver your #1 priority, your X project."

"No, taking that action would risk violating regulatory or legal requirements the firm has committed to comply with."

However, when delivering "no," provide a **time frame or discuss alternatives.** For example:

"No, we're unable to get it done this week with our existing demands, but is there something with a lower priority that we could defer so that we could tackle this now for you?"

"No, that action would violate the company's policy, but there are two other actions we could take that might be just as effective. Let me tell you about them..."

#3: Look for Opportunities To Over-Deliver

Once you know what they value, it's time to kick butt and deliver -- and over-deliver where you can. Over-delivering is the process of keeping your word, going the extra mile, and giving your client even MORE than they expected. This is one of the most essential strategies you can embrace when working with your key clients.

That said, it's impossible to over-deliver 100% of the time. Some things don't require it. But doing it at select opportunities will elevate your reputation and turn your clients into raving fans.

Here are some examples of what this looks like:

Give them 25% more than they were expecting.
If they were expecting you to deliver three resumes for candidates for their Finance Director vacancy, don't just do a resume drop. Instead, go beyond this and provide your personalized, bullet-pointed insights. In these insights, highlight the strengths and weaknesses of each of these candidates, along with your advice on the best fit. Or provide all this information two days earlier than expected.

Provide 2-3 options or solutions on tough issues.
Clients love having choices when they feel they're limited to one. When this happens, work with them to select and customize the best one(s) to their situation.

For example: Let's say your client is concerned about keeping their best people and wants to throw retention bonus money at them. You can either say no and fight them on it. Or you can say yes but over-deliver by improving this solution. How? By getting your client to agree that as part of the deal, both of you will develop an overall retention strategy which might include: (1) enriching their jobs, (2) providing more visibility and recognition for their accomplishments, (3) prioritizing their work and (4) providing greater work-life flexibility. You've now delivered beyond expectations by making the retention bonus part of a much

larger, multi-pronged solution that will likely drive retention up-
wards.

Develop helpful tools clients can use without you.
Many clients enjoy being self-directed. Provide webinars, online
training, or one-page cheat sheets on common issues like interviewing, rewarding performance, leadership, calibrating
performance ratings, retaining talent, improving engagement, or
giving feedback.

Having these ready-to-use tools when coaching your clients --
or available online so that your clients can access them anytime
will label you as a hero in their eyes.

Become their trusted advisor.
This involves becoming the person your client can confide in, say
anything to, and let their hair down with – anytime. Unfortunately, this typically doesn't happen overnight because it involves
gaining from your client a precious commodity that is generally
only gained with time, which is…*trust.*

**However, Sometimes Trust CAN Be Acquired
Quickly If You Can Spot A Vexing Pain Point
…And Help Your Client Address It.**

That is exactly what Catherine Weller did.

Catherine was highlighted in the best-selling book, *Influenc-
ing Without Authority.*

At the time, she was an HR manager in a manufacturing division of a high-tech company. She was supporting a frustrated
division General Manager who despised the HR function and just
about everyone in it.

And with his direct report team, this GM constantly com-
plained about their lack of initiative. But yet, he was blind to his
own part in contributing to their passivity.

At the meetings he ran, he would frustrate his group by con-
tinually asking for input, but then he'd ignore it and do things his
own way.

And though his team quietly chuckled about it, this had begun negatively and noticeably affecting their morale over time.

Catherine believed that if she could get him to recognize that his behavior sent the wrong message to his people, he would be a far more effective leader.

However, being new to the organization, she was reluctant to confront him because she was concerned about his immense pride, quick temper, and perceived resistance to feedback about his leadership style. In addition, she thought he might also certainly resist any advice from her, a more junior member of the hated HR group.

Undaunted, she decided to approach him anyway in terms of a currency she knew he valued: time.

She asked him if he was satisfied with how his meetings were going, and he confirmed he was not. Then she said she knew of a way to save time and speed up the decisions made in his meetings.

This caught his attention.

He opened up and began to discuss his take on the issue with her. And that allowed her to suggest tactfully that she thought he was inadvertently making the problem worse -- and she provided him with a couple of compelling examples.

To her surprise, he agreed with her observations and confessed he'd like some help. They immediately started planning his meetings together and debriefing them afterward.

Although he never became an outstanding meeting leader, he worked hard to break his self-defeating pattern of ignoring his team's input and suggestions – and instead allowed several of his team's ideas to be implemented. When the team saw that the GM was trying, everyone jumped in, and the overall team became more engaged and productive.

Most importantly to Catherine, the GM was extremely grateful to her and saw her (and HR) in a brand new light – as a REAL partner and trusted advisor. He continued planning and debriefing meetings with her and then provided even more opportunities for her to have more impact as his HR leader.

Like Catherine, you can gain trust quickly by taking note of the *real* priorities of your client leaders and seizing the opportunity to help them address them. **Often, you will find that these are personal issues. They're about the client and their *behavior, not necessarily* the business.**

And going the extra mile on these types of issues is how you can over-deliver in your HR support.

#4: Spend Time on Their Turf Regularly.

I learned this lesson the hard way when I moved into the VP HR role supporting the supply chain organization in the second-largest division of PepsiCo. In this position, I had accountability for 21 field locations plus the supply chain executives at the division headquarters.

My assumption was -- since I had HR managers and directors reporting to me at each of the locations -- that I could stay in touch with them virtually by phone, email, and through written updates. This would enable me to focus most of my attention on the higher-ups at division HQ.

HUGE mistake.

I made two terrible workforce decisions because I spent my first six weeks in my office -- not in the field where most of my new clients resided. And as a result, I was not in touch with the REAL workforce issues there. So when those two critical decisions I made blew up, I was embarrassed personally, and all fingers pointed directly at me.

I knew immediately that I was one more bad decision away from getting fired.

So, with no choice, I proactively changed my approach. I re-allocated my time and re-set expectations with everyone. I'd now spend 60% of my time (three days a week) in the field where 90% of my clients resided. To help me handle the execs at headquarters while I was away, I also promoted my best HR leader as their contact so they'd not feel neglected.

This worked like a charm.

My new routine would go something like this: a week or so in advance, I'd pick out a couple of days to visit one of the field locations. "Hey, I'm planning to come out on Tuesday and Wednesday. You in town those days? I'd like to stop in and check things out."

That's how I'd fill out my calendar.

When I'd arrive, I'd meet with the HR leader first, then we'd walk the plant floor, and say hello to as many hourly associates as I could shake hands with without disrupting productivity. I'd chat with the associates about their issues, not HR's. If the place was unionized, we met with the union leaders too. Everyone was initially suspicious about the new corporate HR guy, but things warmed up as I made more visits.

I'd often get pulled into an office for an impromptu discussion about the big workforce problem of the day. Then I'd spend the rest of the time with the HR leader, General Manager, Plant Director, or the business leaders at the site, rolling up my sleeves and problem-solving that issue or other talent-related problems they couldn't resolve at headquarters.

After a day or two, I'd often leave with a lengthy to-do list of action items to follow-up on. And they held me accountable for them -- *which was fantastic!*

More importantly, I was never again seen as an out-of-touch bureaucrat. Or blindsided. And my visits became anticipated, welcomed, and highly productive...*because they saw me as a partner and source of help.* Through these proactive visits, I learned some critical lessons:

- No matter where they reside, book time on your calendar to visit folks on *their turf* regularly -- whether they're in the next office or in the next time zone. Set up even routine meetings, where possible, with your clients *in their* office, not yours.
- Take time to connect regularly, when things are going well. That way, your presence doesn't raise suspicions when things blow up.
- Finally, even if you don't have a specific reason to see your clients -- create one.

The power of your physical presence is immense and builds stronger bridges and relationships with your clients. Face time (especially on significant issues) often trumps numerous phone calls, e-mails, and texts.

#5: Deepen Your Knowledge of the Business.

Obviously, acquiring business knowledge doesn't stop with what we covered in Rule #3 (Know the Business Cold & How Your HR Role Fits). In addition, you should regularly update your **Strategic Focus document,** as was suggested in that chapter.

But that's just a start.

The more you can deepen your knowledge of your clients' business and operating demands, the better you can deliver the HR solutions they need. Along these lines, here are some specific actions to add to your onboarding plan and calendar:

Climb into the bowels of the business.
I alluded to some of this earlier, but let me expand on this idea because it's so important.

- Set aside time to visit your factories, distribution centers, call centers, sales offices or customer service locations to beef up your end-to-end knowledge of how the product or service is created and delivered.
- Spend a day with a sales person when they call on their customer accounts. Any account will work, but *top account* sales calls or visits are especially instructive. Listen to the customer's issues and how the sales person approaches and interacts with them.
- Drop by your R&D facilities to discover how products and services are researched, tested, and commercialized.
- Listen in on your consumer complaints group while consumer issues or problems are being addressed.
- Attend marketing presentations to find out how new offerings are being branded, pitched, and differentiated in the marketplace.

All of this will give you a personal first-hand experience with the business that you can draw on when discussing HR issues with your clients.

Get your name on the essential distribution lists.
Most clients distribute monthly financial results, market analyst reports, strategic reviews, competitor news, or legislative and regulatory updates.

Put yourself on these lists (often, it's the same for everyone). If the data is good enough for your business leaders, it's good enough for you.

If you find it difficult to get copied on these lists, ask your business leader, general manager, or your boss to make the request for you.

Improve your financial intelligence.
Take time to enlarge your network to include Finance. However, you don't have to bug the crap out of your CFO. Instead, find a financial analyst who helps pull the numbers that show how your client's business is performing.

Lunch and learn with them. Get their coaching on how your business makes money. Build a relationship. Offer to return the favor by becoming a resource to them on HR issues.

Tune in on earnings calls.
If you're in a publicly traded company, listen to the quarterly earnings call with the analysts...especially the Q&A segment at the end of the call. Or read the transcripts. It's an excellent way to get a recap of the strategic story your company is telling and gain insights on what investors – and your business leaders — are both excited and worried about.

While you're tuning into calls, note the role played by the folks in the Investor Relations group. They are the key story tellers who have to explain to the analysts and shareholders everything from the quarterly earnings to the latest SEC filing to the most current products or services provided by the organization. When they're not scrambling to meet a disclosure deadline,

schedule a working lunch with one of them to understand the big picture. Pay for their meal. It's time and money well spent.

Summary & Action Steps

Delivering value to your clients is the main reason your HR leadership role and your team were created in the first place. And there's no way to provide real value and satisfy your clients without knowing **what matters** to them and committing to their agenda.

Act on the following **five strategies** to build your credibility and turn your clients into raving fans.

1. Start with an early listening tour.
2. Identify the client priorities you will act on.
3. Look for opportunities to over-deliver.
4. Spend time on their turf,
5. Deepen your knowledge of the business.

As you're doing this, take some time to update your **Strategic Focus document** (Rule #3) based on your new insights.

* * *

Rule #8:
CLARIFY EXPECTATIONS
UP, DOWN & ALL AROUND

Getting crystal clear on what's expected of you is one of the most important things you can do to get off to a great start. And it's one of the easiest things to neglect.

You may think this is unimportant if you have *verbally discussed* this topic with your boss already and are satisfied that you know what's expected.

I'm sorry, that's only a start. And it's not enough for the longer-term. I strongly recommend taking verbal understanding a step further and doing the following.

#1: Agree On A Set Of Written Performance Goals.

Discussing and *documenting* your performance goals is the best way of ensuring that you, your boss, and your clients are aligned and stay aligned. **This is Critical Boss Conversation #5 – referenced in Rule #6.**

Here are some additional reasons you want to have this conversation with your boss and your key clients:

- **It minimizes surprises at performance review time.** These days, every organization handles the performance review process differently. Most still have formal goal setting, year-end reviews, and ongoing feedback against performance throughout the year. However, some firms have moved away from form-al systems or have trashed the review process entirely. No matter what your organization is doing, by taking the lead to align and document your performance expectations with your boss, you safely minimize the risk of surprise whenever the time comes to discuss your overall performance.

- **It helps you deal with complexity.** Matrix organizations are alive and well in many large, globally complex organizations. For example, you might have two bosses or a stronger dotted-line boss than you thought when you were hired. Or you may have accountabilities that have drastically expanded. Or there may be targets committed to by your predecessor that weren't clear at the time you were brought aboard that you'll now be expected to meet. All of these situations reinforce the need to capture one set of written performance expectations that all relevant parties can agree on.

- **It permits you to gain immense clarity from other key stakeholders besides your boss.** For example, if you support business leaders or have one or multiple dotted-line bosses, you can include objectives that address their critical needs and key expectations.

- **It allows you to adapt to rapid changes.** Business and HR priorities change. Clients change. Your boss might move on. A written set of objectives will enable you to modify them to stay current and aligned with the differing needs of a new incoming boss or changes in your client group.

- **Finally, it allows you to clarify expectations for your team.** This is probably the most important benefit. Having your expectations on paper will enable you to align your team's objectives with yours. Distributing a copy of your performance goals is a powerful way to build your team and gain agreement on their performance.

So documenting expectations is crucial.

It's so crucial that if your boss doesn't take the initiative on this, then you should step up, take charge and craft some performance objectives yourself for their feedback and buy-in. Again, this is the best way to get on the same page and prevent misunderstandings later.

Further, I recommend developing objectives that adhere to the S.M.A.R.T. formula. That is establishing goals that are: Specific, Measurable, Achievable and Realistic with Time Frames for achieving them.

Here are some actual examples to illustrate:

As the site's HR leader, spearhead initiatives to improve employee engagement by 12 percentage points and increase the site's ranking from #12 to at least #9 among the 16 food manufacturing locations.
(HR Manager at a manufacturing location).

Lead the introduction of a new incentive plan for the Midwest sales region by August 1. This effort should be done in collaboration with the Sales Leadership Team and should lead to an improvement in the retention of key talent (at a rate to be determined).
(Manager – Total Rewards)

Working with the VP of Customer Service, cut the cost-to-hire rate of entry-level customer service reps by 15% by the end of the fiscal year -- through improvements in using social media and other innovations to attract candidates.
(Senior Director – Talent Acquisition).

Based on senior leadership feedback, lead the initiative to consolidate the corporate Talent Review and Performance Review processes resulting in less duplication of data and a reduction of 14 hours of review time per manager -- without any loss of essential information.
(VP-Talent Management & Organization Development)

THE NEW HR LEADER'S FIRST 100 DAYS —

Again, these are merely illustrative samples to give you a flavor. This doesn't mean that every single objective you set should be S.M.A.R.T. It simply means that you should **try to clarify expectations and craft measurable objectives and targets whenever possible.**

With all this done, it's time for you to...

#2: Re-Set Performance Expectations For Your Direct Report Team.

As alluded to earlier, now that you have your own objectives, you'll want to re-establish and clarify expectations with your staff so everyone is on the same page and that your team members know how their performance ties to what you're trying to achieve.

Ideally, these should be SMART objectives, too, just like those you established with your boss. **Sequentially, you should *set* yours first, distribute a copy to them, and then make sure that each team member's objectives support and align with yours.**

#3: Start Holding Your Team Accountable.

Once you've established performance expectations, you've laid the foundation to hold your team members accountable. This is an essential ingredient in taking charge and building your credibility.

There are many ways to accomplish this:

Commit to consistent one-on-one meetings.
Meet weekly or bi-weekly with your direct reports. Yes, this seems like a considerable amount of time. And yes, this may not be sustainable if you have a huge team. But, in your first 100 days, it's too early to know who needs time with you, how often and how long.

If you have a massive amount of direct reports, it's better to meet for a shorter time (20-30 minutes) with each one every couple of weeks than going too long between meetings.

Ask them to come in ready to talk about the following:

- Their top few priorities (this week, this quarter)
- Challenges and obstacles they're encountering and how they're handling them
- Opportunities they spot in their role or for the team
- What they need from you

Occasionally, set aside time to ask about the big picture -- what they enjoy and don't, what they want to learn next, or how they see their career developing. Then follow up on any action items coming from this meeting.

Hold regular meetings for the entire team.

When you attend a church, synagogue, temple, or mosque, you don't need to call each weekend to find out what time the service is being held.

Hold your weekly or bi-weekly meetings the same way – same day/time, same location, same dial-in number – so it becomes a consistent, calendar-blocked priority. However, don't meet just for the sake of meeting. Instead, use these sessions to discuss or get input on key issues vital to the team.

Also, be on time. This is essential during your first three months. It sends the message to your team that they're important and that delivering commitments on time is also crucial.

Step in and begin correcting performance issues.

When you don't do this once you've laid down performance expectations, two issues arise:

a) The direct report who isn't accountable likely knows they're not doing what is expected of them and therefore doesn't respect you for your failure to hold them responsible.

b) All the other team members likely know this person isn't doing what they're supposed to do, either. And they know you're not holding this person accountable and therefore don't respect you either.

Finally, if that's not enough, the accountability of other team members *will* go south when they know you're not confident enough to deal with this type of conflict.

Build on what is going well.
Seek out good performance wherever it occurs, however small – and acknowledge it. Such appreciation will be welcomed as long as it is genuine and honest.

Along these lines, seek out your team's opinions. Listen to their ideas. Develop your staff as a group of allies. Involve them in key decisions and let them guide and help you through your initial period of taking charge until you get more comfortable in your new role.

Address team conflicts swiftly.
At some point, your direct reports are going to fight amongst themselves. It's inevitable.

Team conflicts must be confronted swiftly. Rifts in a team can turn toxic quickly if left unchecked. Unfortunately, you may not even realize there is an issue until it's too late. So uncover conflicts early through consistent one-on-ones and candid team meetings so you are not caught off guard.

If personality conflicts arise, direct the parties to work it out themselves. If they can't, and it impacts the team's productivity, bring them together to discuss it. Aim to clear the air and come to an understanding without placing blame. Let them know it's fine to disagree respectfully. The key word is *respectfully.*

Finally, use this to set your expectations about respect, how the team should work together, and how conflicts should be handled in the future.

Finally, plan any major team building carefully.
It is tempting to launch off-site or full-day team-building activities, such as HR visioning, strategy development and big-time

brainstorming sessions right away. New HR leaders with a consensus-building style often are eager to take their group offsite to build relationships and tap into the insights of the total team.

While this is admirable, it also poses a danger.

Doing this too soon strengthens your team's bonds, which is usually a good thing -- EXCEPT if you know that you'll be terminating some key team members shortly. If so, you may have to repeat this event all over again to rebuild the team after all the bloodletting has concluded.

This does NOT mean, of course, that you should avoid meeting as a group. You should, and regularly.

It just means you should think carefully about doing any major off-site teambuilding if you know you'll be making major changes in the composition of your team. You may just want to delay this until the full team you want is in place. *(To help you consider the key actions you may want to take before planning your offsite event, skip ahead and read through Rule #11 and Rule #13).*

Summary & Action Steps

Gaining agreement on performance expectations is the foundation for your first 100 days and future success.

1. Don't hesitate to take charge, step up to the plate and **put your performance expectations in writing.**

2. Then **get approval** from your boss, your dotted-line boss (if one exists), and your clients.

Once you're clear on your own, then **align the expectations of your direct report team to yours** and then **begin holding them accountable.**

* * *

Rule #9:
CUT YOUR HR LEARNING CURVE IN HALF

Leverage This Powerful Tool To Close
Your HR Knowledge Gaps Quickly!

In your new role, you'll be on a learning curve -- no matter how many years of HR leadership experience you have or how much you think you already know.

Here's why. Every organization delivers HR differently. As a result, HR practices, policies, systems, and metrics can vary drastically, even across similar organizations. And the quicker you can master those in the new organization, the faster you'll be able to gear up your performance.

This is where the **HR Onboarding Accelerator** checklist tool can help you.

It is *Best Practice Tool #9.1* at the end of this chapter. To get a feel for it, check it out now.

As you'll see, this tool defines what you must <u>learn</u>, <u>know</u> and <u>master</u> about your new company's unique HR practices, policies, and metrics.

It consists of a checklist of 60 items that will **speed up your onboarding time and save you hours of wasted effort** by giving you basic yet essential information necessary for mastering your new role. You'll also find an optional part B section covering HR metrics.

The best way to gather this information fast is by arranging a meeting with your new boss (or a trusted colleague or advisor). Share this checklist with them and then ask WHERE and WHO can provide you with the information for each item.

Even better, if you already have an admin, assistant, intern or chief of staff who supports you, assign this to them and have them gather and review the information with you.

One caution: This checklist is very detailed and goes deep, but not all items will apply. Some additional tips:

- For HR generalists, the first 20-35 items are the most critical to grasp early. For others, it will vary.
- Everything won't apply to your role. So feel free to drop or add some items from this list.
- For ease of use, you may want to download a copy of these pages to **edit them to fit your specific situation.**

You should plan to get this checklist completed in your **first month** on the job. That said, it is described in detail in the following few pages.

* * *

New HR Leader
Best Practice Tool 9.1:
THE HR ONBOARDING
ACCELERATOR

You can also download a copy of this tool as a word
doc at → **http://SuccessInHR.com/leader-807191**
(This is in a .zip file. If you have any issues downloading
this file, email me at alan@successinhr.com.)

**Here is your checklist of the HR-related information you
should compile, have quick access to, know or master…**

*__Note:__ For HR generalists, the first 20-35 items
are the most critical to grasp early. For those
in HR specialist roles, it varies.*

**#1: List of all current employees that comprise your client
group (including all leaders and non-leaders).** This list should
contain:

- Their locations and hire dates
- Current annual salaries and wages
- Bonus targets (if applicable)
- Sales commission targets (if applicable)
- Years of service with the Company
- Highest educational degree and prior experience,
- If available. Include annual stock option run-rate, if applicable
- Indicate the last review date if you are on an anniversary review. If on an annual review, indicate the last date and average increase.
- Identify any accrued vacation time per employee. Identify key employees on the list (asterisk or label "key").

**#2: How much HR data or employee-related information is
readily available online?**

- Where is the HR portal, company intranet, or internal website?
- Does it contain current and accurate electronic personnel records on all employees?
- What additional talent, workforce, and employee-related data is contained within it?
- Where is it located? How can it be accessed quickly?
- Who is responsible for maintaining it?
- What information is confidential, and what isn't?

#3: How does communication happen within the organization?

- What *offline methods* (voicemail, meetings, monthly team gatherings, quarterly meetings, etc.) and *online media* (e.g., email, text, daily newsletters, company-wide webinars, etc.) are most often used?
- What's the quickest way to gain access to and use these channels of communication?

#4: Job descriptions (or at least brief position profiles) for all major job categories in your client organization. This should include the minimum education and experience levels required. If any unique skill sets are needed, these should also be noted.

#5: Current pay ranges and the current merit increase matrix (if available). These should be included if there are multiple ranges or different ranges for different geographical locations.

#6: Gather all formal company-wide talent review and people planning documents for the HR processes below – including a detailed description of how these processes work:

- Annual Employee Performance Review Process
- Talent Review Process
- Succession Planning Process
- HR Strategic Plan (corporate, division, and for your unit)

#7: From the above people planning processes, gather the previous year's actual results for your client group. Also, make note of the following for your client group:
- High potential employees
- Back-ups/successors for key positions
- Diversity and inclusion issues & challenges
- Problem performers
- Key strategic HR priorities and short-term areas of focus

#8: Employee departures. A list of individuals who have left the organization in the last twelve months – including their:
- The last position.
- Length of service with the Company prior to termination
- Any severance payments or liabilities incurred.
- If known, indicate whether an employee took a position with an affiliated company.
- Identify key employees (or regretted losses) on the list (asterisk or label "key").

#9: Employee turnover data for the last two years.
- Break out two lists: one for those who voluntarily left; and the other for those who were involuntarily terminated with the reasons why.

#10: Is the company an at-will employer? Is a formal Discipline or Discharge policy in place, and is it progressive?

#11: The formal or informal processes used for department transfers, out-of-cycle promotions, new hire requisitions, performance reviews, etc.
- Forms used and indicate if electronic or manual.
- Describe the approval process for each of the above and whether additional signatures are required.

#12: How is the Staffing or Talent Acquisition function performed?

- In house?
- Outside consultants?
- Search firms?
- Who is the main contact for this function?

#13: Is there an HR Learning, Training, OD, or Leadership Development function?
- What types of learning initiatives and training programs are offered to employees?
- What types of leadership development or OD services are provided to employees?
- Who is the primary contact for this function?

#14: The corporate culture – open, team-based environment, top-down decision-making process, etc. Is there an everyday dress code or dress-down days?

#15: Is there an Employee Relations function, ombudsman, or facilitator role? Who performs this?

#16: For all unionized facilities: All labor contracts, collective bargaining agreements, contract expiration dates, and any consents, waivers, or amendments.

#17: For all non-union facilities: Documents that describe the plan or strategy for remaining union-free. Also, data about any union's recent/past organizing drives, the unions involved, petitions filed with the NLRB, red-yellow-green employee analysis, etc.

#18: Reductions in Force (RIFs) in the prior year. How many employees were involved, their locations, and the severance benefits provided under each activity? Have any fallen under the WARN Act?

#19: If there are multiple work shifts, what are the shifts (day, swing, graveyard) and include the shift differential for each.

#20: Is there an on-site cafeteria, vending machines, etc? Are free coffee, soft drinks, etc., provided? Are these provided at all locations? If not, why not?

#21: A description of the payroll process, including who processes paychecks. Provide the vendor name if payroll is processed externally) and include:

- Frequency of paycheck distribution (list time frames; i.e., monthly, every two weeks, on the 1st and 16th, etc.).
- Also, indicate the frequency and timing of commission payouts (monthly, every two months, etc.) and whether it differs from the normal payroll processing.

#22: Employment contracts (or employment-related documented commitments or agreements) with current or former employees. Include any severance agreements triggered by a "change in control."

#23: Employment contracts (if you have international clients). If contracts are not in English, they should be translated. Again, include any special severance agreements.

#24: Existing employee policies: pay plans, employee handbooks or policy manuals, etc. Include any supervisory or manager handbooks and existing company rules and regulations.

#25: All vacation, sick pay, paid time off, holiday, sabbaticals, and other employment policies. For each, include:

- Eligibility and accrual rates
- Days accrued and how they are monitored.
- If carry-over is allowed, please include and indicate maximums, if any.

- If any class of employees is treated differently (non-exempts, executives, etc.), please indicate the specific policies that apply to each.

#26: Sales commission or incentive plans. For each employee on commission, include the commission plan agreement or description. If such don't exist, include target commission amounts per employee.

#27: Other compensation incentive plans:
- If there are other incentive plans for a select group of employees, include a description of who is eligible.
- If there are multiple plans, include each separately.
- If an employee is eligible for multiple plans (i.e., commission plus bonus), please include and indicate who is affected.

#28: Profit-sharing plans. This should include the actual policy detailing eligibility, payout requirements, and payout amounts.

#29: Stock option plan. This should include when options are granted (for new hires, at review time, for promotions, discretionary, etc.).
- If a matrix is used for granting stock, please include if grants vary for International employees.
- Include the information specific to the International sites.
- Also include the typical vesting schedule for options.
- Indicate if vesting differs given whether the stock is New Hire or renewal.
- How is the stock granted (for one year out, Evergreen, renewal stock, etc.)?

#30: Stock Purchase Program…include the SPP plan document and indicate the purchase period time frames, cost to the employee, etc.

#31: Loan provision for stock option exercises? If so, include who is eligible.

#32: Identify the specific broker who processes stock transactions. Include the commission rates charged. Is the same broker used for International transactions? Does anything vary Internationally?

#33: Other employee perks. This should include descriptions of all relevant documentation, including plan documents or employee communications. If there are programs other than those listed above, please include:

- Bonus
- Company car
- Housing and relocation
- Incentive plans
- Deferred compensation arrangements
- Jury duty, bereavement leave
- Personal time off
- Educational assistance
- Tuition reimbursement
- Employee recognition
- Community service programs
- Service awards
- Executive perquisites

#34: If any such plans still exist, gather any qualified retirement and pension plans. This should include the most recent actuarial report showing assumptions; include all reports, applications, or information filed with any government agency or distributed to plan participants and their beneficiaries for the welfare plans, pension plans, and the other related plans.

#35: Defined contribution plans (401k, etc.). This should clarify if the plan provides for an employer match and the history of any employer match to date. For highly compensated employees, have they had their contributions restricted? Provide the latest information showing the most recent ADP/ACP testing.

#36: Does the 401(k) have a loan provision? Determine employees or past employees who may have an outstanding loan.

#37: How many stock or investment funds can employees invest in? What are the names of the funds? Who manages the funds? Please provide all plan documents and communications to employees.

#38: Employee health care plans (including medical, dental, vision, prescription, dependent care, elder care, life insurance, AD&D insurance, short- and long-term disability, flexible spending accounts [FSAs]) and provide plan descriptions. Describe eligibility requirements, employer rates, employee rates, deductibles, maximum out-of-pocket expenses, and total employees covered by the plan (i.e., medical plan -- HMO, PPO, and EPO).

If executives are treated differently... clarify differences from a plan perspective and any cost differential. If the Company picks up the additional costs, please indicate. If the Plans differ on a site-to-site basis, include information for each location.

#39: Dates that each of the health care plans is up for renewal.

#40: All employees and their dependents that are currently on or eligible for COBRA. It should indicate for which plans they are electing coverage and the COBRA cost for each plan. In addition, indicate the COBRA coverage start date and maximum end date.

#41: The last two years Form 5500's for any qualified health and welfare benefit plans.

#42: The Business Travel Accident policy and plan document. Include when the Plan is up for renewal.

#43: Non-qualified plan documents and a **list of participants** under each plan.

#44: Insurance policies/contracts associated with any matter described above.

#45: Any employee controversies or investigations (with or by the OFCCP or any government agency, provider or any beneficiary) involving the operation or qualification of, or payment of benefits under, any pension or welfare plan or other employment matters. This should include claims or any potential liability relating to employment, compensation, benefits, discrimination, possible violations of and other employment-related claims, and litigation of any kind under any Federal, State, local, or foreign law, regulation, or decision.

#46: Employees on VISA and their current status – including those being company-sponsored for permanent residency.

#47: Complaints regarding compliance by the Company with any immigration laws.

#48: Last two years EEO-1 and Veterans reports.

#49: Federal, state, and local compliance agreements. Descriptions of all other employee grievances, unfair labor practices, employee disputes, or employment terminations.

#50: Documentation relating to actual financial experience (claims experience, premiums paid, etc.) under the welfare benefit plans described above. If there are international locations, include their financial experience as appropriate.

#51: Reports filed with any governmental agency relating to occupational safety and health issues for the prior two years.

#52: Employees currently on a Leave of Absence – including leave reason, the beginning date of leave, anticipated return date, and any other pertinent detail.

#53: Employees or plan beneficiaries hospitalized on a long-term basis, receiving disability, workers compensation, or similar payments and any outstanding issues. Include name, disability status, the beginning of disability, anticipated end date, any follow-up status, etc.

#54: Any unusual arrangements with employees, including health maintenance or preferred provider organization participation or affirmative action plans.

#55: Individuals not considered employees who have been providing their services to the Company on an ongoing basis (e.g. consultants, search firms, etc.). Include the following: the work performed, agreed upon payment for services (hourly or contractual amount), the start of the agreement, the projected end of the agreement, and whether a specific fee has been agreed to whether or not the services are performed (i.e., a set fee for 6-months).

#56: Is there current and accurate I-9 data and related back up data on each employee? Is it maintained separate for the corporate personnel records?

#57: Discrimination complaints against the Company or any predecessor during the last 5 years. Include the date of claims, persons involved, and actual or expected outcome.

#58: Claims, lawsuits, arbitrations, or other proceedings (including administrative and arbitrage proceedings and government agency investigations) which are pending or threatened. Including copies of any related documentation.

#59: Pending local, state, or federal legislation or regulatory rulings or processes, which might have a material adverse impact on the Company's business, assets, or customer relationships.

#60: All consent decrees, judgments, orders, administrative determinations, or arbitrage awards requiring, prohibiting, or limiting any future activities of the Company or which have not been fully satisfied. Include copies of each.

*   *   *

Optional Part B:
Basic Key HR Metrics

If they exist, you may also want to gather essential HR metrics on the workforce/clients you support.

If such measures don't exist, this represents a massive opportunity for you to begin capturing this data to *establish a baseline from which you can work with your clients to drive improvements (and prove your value).*

You only need to track and improve **3 or 4 key metrics** to make a difference. Here are a few examples to consider:

Recruitment / Talent Attraction
1. What percent of hires remain after two years of being hired?
2. Which selection criteria are the best predictors of high performance in the first year and beyond?
3. Which selection criteria are the best predictors of retaining top-performing talent?
4. What is the percent of offers are accepted by the top talent?

Retention
1. What percent of the total employees are retained each year? (overall retention %).
2. What percent of the high performers/high potentials are retained each year? (top talent retention %).
3. What percent of exits is voluntary versus involuntary?
4. What are the reasons that people voluntarily leave?
5. From what jobs and leaders do the voluntary leavers tend to depart?

Development
1. What percent of promotions come from inside versus outside the firm?
2. How does the individual performance after training compare with performance before training?
3. Which employee groups benefit most from training (e.g., level, age, experience, nationality)?

Succession
1. What percent of critical (or key at-risk) positions have ready-now backup candidates?
2. What percent of the ready-now backup candidates are actually moved into positions?

Total Rewards
1. What is the correlation of pay increases with improvements in performance? Retention?
2. Which form of compensation (base pay, bonus, stock, incentive pay) results in the most significant short-term and long-term performance?

Employee Engagement
1. What percent of employees know and can describe the company's mission, long-term objectives, and business strategy?

2. What percent of employees know and can describe the company's external brand identity, and what differentiates it in the marketplace?
3. What percent of employees perform above and beyond the scope of their job description and deliver added value?

*　*　*

Rule #10:
DECIPHER THE REAL
CULTURE OF THE ORGANIZATION

You should invest as much time learning the organization's culture as you do developing your knowledge of the business and its unique HR practices.

Said differently, knowing "what" to do is not enough. You must also know "how" to get things done within the personality and fabric of your organization.

Many organizations have complex cultures that are tough to figure out. And making wrong assumptions or attempting to launch new HR initiatives without assessing their "cultural fit" first can lead to painful, embarrassing mistakes later.

Don't fall into this avoidable trap.

There are various ways to get a read on your culture. **But let's start with the best approach---which is to pull together an informal advisory network of 3-5 colleagues who can guide and advise you.** If needed, get your boss' assistance in identifying who they are and lining them up. There are three essential roles you need for these individuals to play.

1. **Seasoned Peer Advisor**
2. **Capability Leaders**
3. **Connectors**

Some people can serve in _multiple_ roles. But it would be best if you had all of them covered.

With that in mind, let's discuss the value of these three roles.

Role #1:
The Seasoned Peer Advisor

This is a colleague who can show you the ropes and provide insights on how the formal and informal systems in the organization work. They are a resource to help you understand HR policy issues, the culture, and politics.

They provide insight into buzzwords, the key power players, unspoken cultural norms, and the organization's unwritten rules. Next, they help you learn to speak the language. Finally, they serve as a sounding board as you consider options for implementing your agenda.

The best candidates are folks already on your peer team or other HR leaders at your same level. The ideal person has been in their position at least a year and has recently tackled similar organizational, leadership, and cultural challenges you now face.

A caution: Some of your colleagues may not have previously served as peer advisors and may be caught off guard or unprepared. If that's the case, simply explain that you'd like to leverage their know-how and experience to do your job better. Typically, once they understand the rationale, most people feel incredibly flattered to be able to share their insights.

With your peer advisor, start with one-on-one conversations every few days. **Be ready to drive the discussion.** Bring questions and real-life scenarios to get their opinion and gain insight. They could be questions about cultural norms, unwritten rules, political mistakes to avoid, puzzling clients, or where to find difficult-to-locate data or company information.

Cheryl Allison-Sykes did this when she first arrived in her new senior HR role. Here's how she described her experience...

I was hired as the VP of Employee & Labor Relations at a unionized specialty food company that a private equity firm had just acquired. I was brought in specifically for my eight years of experience in labor relations and my track record in negotiating collective bargaining agreements and dealing effectively with union officials. Unfortunately, I had no food industry experience. My entire career was in the security inustry dealing with electrical workers, which is very different.

I knew right away that my learning curve would be steep. There was a lot I'd have to learn about the culture, the existing relationships between management and the union, and past practices, if I was going to have any impact in the first few months, I was there.

So my boss, the SVP of HR, partnered me up with the former labor relations director of the company, a veteran with ten years of experience, who had taken a lucrative early retirement package offered by the private equity folks.

He had done a great deal of work over the years dealing with those exact unions and management teams I was now responsible for. Because he was treated so well by the acquiring company, he was thrilled to share his insights and coaching with me.

And they were invaluable.

We had roughly six extensive two- to three-hour working sessions in my first two months. I had lots of questions. And he had great answers, phenomenal insights, and sage wisdom. I learned from many of his previous mistakes that he readily shared with me. ***He also served as a resource and sounding board for me by phone, email, and text when sticky labor issues arose.***

As a result, I got off to a terrific start and was able to get results immediately. And within my first four months, I led the contract negotiations with one of our three major unions, resulting in a lucrative agreement for the company that improved our manufacturing flexibility well below our budgeted costs.

Senior management was highly impressed and pleased with these accomplishments. And I ended up looking pretty damned knowledgeable and established credibility early with everyone, including the union officials.

I wouldn't have accomplished these results without my peer advisor.

Clearly, Cheryl's advisor served in multiple roles and contributed greatly to her success.

Take a page out of her book. The cultural issues you face in your new organization can be subtle and nuanced. No one may tell you you're off-base or barking up the wrong tree. Instead, you may only get a clue or shades of feelings.

Peer advisors like the one Cheryl used can help you validate and get a GPS reading on these situations. And are indispensable in helping you navigate and become more perceptive -- until you get your footing.

That said, let's move on to...

Role #2:
Capability Leaders

These are specialists or technical experts who know how the key business and HR systems work. What kinds of systems?

It could be the HR information system. Or the compensation system. Or the financial and budgeting systems. Or the strategic planning system. Or, frankly, any system the organization has put in place to help drive compliance with their routine, regulatory or standardized practices.

Since no one is an expert on all of these systems, you'll need to recruit multiple capability leaders. As walking fountains of knowledge, these people can beef up your understanding of their particular system and help cut through the complexity.

Question these experts often, but don't just call them when you're stuck. Build relationships with them. Buy them lunch to pick their brain from time to time. In return, be sure to share your resources and experiences, too.

Finally, let's wrap up with...

Role #3:
Connectors

These are the people who seem to know everyone in the organization. Through their extensive network, they can open doors and connect you with others who can help drive your agenda forward and get things done.

Great connectors have terrific people skills and will be eager to put you in touch with others who share similar interests and goals. They typically have active schedules and calendars that are constantly booked. But don't fear. The connector will always squeeze you in.

Now That You Know Who You Need In Your Informal Advisory Network, Assess What You Have.

If you're assuming a new HR role in your current organization, ask yourself if your existing network can provide the support you require. Don't assume that people who have been helpful in the past will continue to be in your new situation. You will encounter different problems, which means some former advisors may not be as relevant in your new role.

Keep in mind that as you move into more senior HR roles, the need for good cultural and political counsel increases dramatically.

Once you've identified the individuals you need, reach out and connect. Ask them for a short phone chat or coffee meeting to get the ball rolling.

With all this in mind, let me give you a bonus.

To supplement your advisory network, here are…

Four More Ideas to Help You Figure Out the Organization.

Idea #1: Tap into internal diversity and inclusion networks, affinity, and employee resource groups.

Many organizations have separate resource or affinity groups for African Americans, Asian Americas, Hispanics, older workers, workers with disabilities, LGBTQ+ employees, women, white males, members of religious denominations, global networks, and others.

However, these groups are diverse and open to all employees at any level. The best groups have a company-recognized charter, purpose, schedule of activities, and meet often. As a result, they play an essential role in retaining talent, connecting those with similar backgrounds and ethnicities, and providing advice in navigating successfully through the organization.

Most members of these groups have no direct connection to HR or your clients – and, as such, can be among your most valuable advisors because they have no horse in your race and can be HR-neutral.

So, pick out a few groups, attend some meetings, and keep your antennae out for members with leadership skills, smarts, and integrity who enjoy talking with you and who you feel would delight in your success.

In addition, they are rare jewels if they have technology expertise, political savvy, or are good at reading the power dynamics within the organization. These types of individuals can serve as tremendous assets in helping you de-puzzle the organization.

Idea #2: Augment your internal network with your own confidants.

Frankly, your advisory network is incomplete without leveraging the people you already trust and have known for years. We all need companions. They are the first people you call, with good or bad news. These are your true confidants that are always there for you. So use them.

While insiders offer many benefits, they cannot be expected to give you a 100% purely objective view of events within your organization. Personal trusted advisors and friends who are outsiders can. They will help you work through emotional issues and decisions you are facing that you may be uncomfortable sharing with any insider. They should be skilled at listening and asking questions, have good insight into how organizations work, and have your best interests at heart.

Idea #3: Never eat alone.

This is the title of a great book by Keith Ferrazzi. It's also an excellent strategy for your first 100 days. Invite someone to lunch every day. These need not be strictly power lunches where you conduct business while trying to keep ketchup off your chin.

Instead, consider lunch an informal, precious block of time that you can use to help you decipher the culture. You have 20 of these golden "opportunities" each month (i.e. 4 workweeks x 5 days each week).

And that means:

- 20 opportunities a month to have lunch with one of your advisors
- 20 opportunities a month to start a new relationship or nurture an existing one
- 20 opportunities a month to deepen your know-how about the business and culture
- 20 opportunities a month to test out a new HR idea that you're thinking about.

Don't waste them. Can't do lunch? An early morning breakfast can accomplish the same purpose.

Idea #4: Hit the happy hours.

This may be an unusual strategy, but hear me out. There is probably a group of people that gather at happy hour on Fridays from time to time. There may be optional celebratory get-togethers. People may have send-off parties for someone's retirement or job change. Consider these opportunities for a good time – and to decipher the culture.

You'll get introduced to people in your company you might otherwise never meet or interact with all the time. In this atmosphere, people let their hair down, and you can use these events to gather knowledge on projects, politics, rumors, and how things get done in the organization.

When attending, engage those you know to gain introductions to those you don't. Avoid asking, "What do you do?" Instead ask, "What's the most interesting thing happening in your world?"

Summary & Action Steps

No HR leader, no matter how capable, can do it alone. You need a network of insiders, outsiders, and trusted advisers to help you navigate through your new culture.

This network is an indispensable resource to help you avoid isolation and losing perspective. To start, select and cultivate three types of advice-givers:

1. The Seasoned Peer Advisor
2. Capability Leaders
3. Connectors

When you find a colleague with one or more of these qualities, foster that relationship because they will become one of your best enablers.

Finally, don't hesitate to block time on your calendar to meet up with colleagues in **diversity and inclusion networks,** at **lunches,** and during **happy hours** to further help you figure out the organization.

* * *

Rule #11:
CUT THE FAT & MUSCLE
UP YOUR TEAM

If you have a large team of direct reports, the most important decision you'll make in your first 100 days will be what to do about them.

Expect to inherit some strong performers, some average ones, and some simply not up to the job. Dave Ulrich, is even more specific about this in his book, *Victory by Organization*. He calls it the 20-60-20 normal distribution of HR professionals.

- 20% are exceptional and deliver real value. You need to stay out of their way and learn from them.
- 20% are laggards, unable or unwilling to use HR to drive business results. You need to not let them deter you.
- 60% are open to learning and making progress towards making an even more significant impact. You want to invest in these folks because they want to and are eager to make a difference.

Obviously, the distribution of your new HR team might vary from the above breakdown. But that's what you must confirm during your first 30 to 60 days.

Specifically, you need to sort out:
- Who's who.
- What roles each individual plays,
- And then make decisions as to *who stays, who to cut* and *what talent to bring in* to muscle up your team.

**That's Exactly What Lilly Dawkins Did When She
Was Hired By A $2 Billion Professional Services
Firm To Be Their New Vice-President Of
Talent Management.**

Lilly was brought in to reestablish the credibility of the firm's six-person Talent Management group, which handled talent acquisition, total rewards, employee relations, and organization development for 1600 professional and executive-level employees.

The perception of her team within the firm was that it was gossipy, untrustworthy, played favorites— and that it was slow in following through on their commitments. From brutally candid conversations with her VP-level clients and boss, Lilly concluded that she didn't have much time to turn this situation around.

After doing her own assessment of her team for four weeks, she quietly engaged a headhunter to recruit potential replacements for two people she didn't think would make the cut. She did this while building relationships and giving everyone on her team the opportunity to succeed.

After six weeks, she was ready to act. She reorganized her group and immediately eliminated two positions. She terminated the director of OD (a person regarded as a "touchy-feely" blabbermouth who couldn't be trusted with confidential information) and the director of talent acquisition (a person who frustrated clients by moving much too slowly in filling critical jobs). She ensured that these two departing people were treated respectfully and received solid severance packages.

She then outsourced talent acquisition to a top-notch contract recruiter, who would report directly to her. And replaced the OD position at a higher (VP) level by bringing in a former, high-potential colleague, who she would be grooming as her successor. These moves strengthened her team and were applauded by her clients.

She kept her other four direct reports. But set a higher, more demanding performance bar for everyone and worked harder to align her team's expectations with those of her business clients.

The road was rough, and one other team member left voluntarily after getting direct feedback from Lilly that, while he was making progress, he wasn't improving fast enough to fit Lilly's new results-driven culture.

Nevertheless, after one year, Lilly got positive feedback on her turnaround and dramatically improved the Talent Management team's reputation (and her own) with her clients.

She learned that it only takes a few key people to drag down the reputation of your entire HR team. And she would also tell you she could have moved a couple of weeks sooner – *probably after four weeks instead of six* – but definitely couldn't have waited any longer than she did.

There is a lesson here for you as well.

When in doubt, have a bias to move quicker on your team than you think you should. The risks of making changes a tad too soon are nothing compared to hit to your reputation of leaving ineffective people in place too long.

And if you're going to cut the fat and muscle up your team, there are three crucial decision points in making such changes: (1) when to do it, (2) how to do it, and (3) avoiding the common traps in the process.

Let's now break each of these decisions down further.

Decision #1:
When to Make Changes in Your Team.

A good rule of thumb: give yourself 30 days to complete a good fact-based assessment of your direct report team. Base this evaluation on feedback from your clients, your boss and most importantly your own first-hand observations of their performance.

Around 30 days but certainly no longer than 60 days, pull the trigger and start making your moves. Moving quickly to reduce the pain will avoid demoralizing your strong performers and provide the kick in the butt that can get the weak performers on track or out the door.

A related key point: If your predecessor left because of poor performance, it is wise to evaluate what role their staff might have played in contributing to their failure.

- If the staff played a significant role, you might need to make changes in the team **even faster** so that the same fate doesn't victimize you.
- If they didn't, you may have the luxury of **more time** to make changes. Remember that success is difficult if your staff cannot provide the horsepower you need to drive your agenda.

Decision #2:
How to Make Changes in Your Team.

Step 1: Establish Your Criteria

You will naturally form early impressions of team members when you arrive. Don't suppress these emotions. Step back and be even more rigorous in your evaluation. This starts with defining some explicit criteria. I've found success using the following:

- **Drive for Results.** Does this team member bring the right kind of passion and enthusiasm to the job, and do their documented performance results evidence this?
- **HR Expertise.** Does this person have the required HR knowledge, skills, and experience needed to do the job effectively?
- **Judgment.** Does this person use good judgment, especially under pressure or when faced with making sacrifices for the greater good?
- **Collaboration.** Does this person have productive client relationships, get along with others on the team, or is they a pain to work with?
- **Trust.** Can you trust this person to keep their word and follow through on projects, assignments, and commitments?

Some criteria may be more important to you than others. To account for this, divide 100 points among these five criteria according to the *relative weight* you place on them.

Again, the above five have worked well for me. Choose your own standards. Having done so, you'll be better positioned to make a more thoughtful and fact-based evaluation.

Step 2: Evaluate Your People

In this step, assess each team member using the weighted criteria you have developed to determine who makes the grade and who doesn't.

Observe, observe, observe.

In your personal interactions and in meetings with your team, notice how the individuals relate to each other and with their clients:

- Do relations with other team members appear cordial and productive? Tense and competitive? Judgmental or reserved?
- Do you detect any alliances? Who defers to whom on a given topic? When one person is speaking, do others roll their eyes or otherwise express disagreement or frustration?
- Pay attention to these signs to test your early insights and detect coalitions and conflicts.

Discuss performance in-depth with each team member.

Depending on your style, these early meetings might be informal, formal, or a combination. But your own preparation and focus should be standardized. During these discussions, you'll want to explore:

- What they are doing well and what could be improved.
- What they do and do not like about their work.
- What they think of your existing strategy and what they could be doing more for the organization, if given the opportunity.

Look for verbal and nonverbal clues.
Note choices of words, body language, and hot buttons.
- Notice what the individual does not say. For example, does the person volunteer information, or do you have to extract it? Does the person take responsibility for problems in their area? Make excuses? Blame others?
- What topics elicit strong emotional responses? These hot buttons provide clues to what motivates the individual and what changes they would be energized by.

Capture good data on their performance.
Examine past performance reviews, work history, and other available work metrics. Couple this with conversations with their former managers, their clients and others familiar with their work.

Step 3: Make the Tough Calls

Using the insights you have gained, assign each team member to one of the following three categories:
- **Keep.** The person is clearly performing well in their current job. They may need some coaching and development down the road, but it's not a big issue. They can also help orient and onboard new team members later.
- **Replace.** The person is not meeting expectations and should be replaced as soon as possible. Options here are termination or transferring them to another department. (*Special caution here:* Transfers should only be considered when the person is a clear misfit for your team but has performed strongly in other roles. Don't establish a reputation for passing on problem performers to other departments).
- **Defer decision for now:** The individual requires further observation and development before reaching a final conclusion. They may also be an adequate performer in a crucial position that is hard-to-replace easily.

Consider all your options.
Letting an employee go can be difficult and time-consuming. Even if poor performance is well documented, the termination process can take weeks, months, or longer. In addition, if there is no paper trail regarding poor performance, it will take time to document.

Fortunately, you do have some alternatives to consider. Often, a poor performer will decide to move on of their own accord in response to a clear message from you.

Alternatively, you can work with your HR/staffing contact to shift the person to a more suitable position if you're genuinely convinced it could work. Again, as mentioned earlier, simply dropping a problem performer on someone else's lap will damage your reputation.

Fill positions wisely.
Who you bring into your team broadcasts more about what's important to you than anything else. Ensure those helping you acquire talent for your team understand the profile of who you need -- not just experience but also attitude and commitment. Let them vet candidates. Then invest your time with the top candidates. Only you can make your best hire.

Treat people respectfully.
Embrace the golden rule. During every phase of your team-restructuring process, treat *everyone* as you would want to be treated. Your direct reports will form lasting impressions of you based on how you manage this part of your job. Even if it's clear to the world that a particular person should be replaced, you will be viewed negatively if you deal with them callously.

Decision #3:
Avoiding Common Traps In Making Changes in Your Team.

Based on the experience of lots of new HR leaders, here are some typical traps to avoid.

Blaming your predecessor for the team you inherited.
This is a common pitfall, especially if the prior leader isn't there and can't defend themselves. And assigning blame to them gives you a convenient excuse. However, the problem is that it's hard to blame your predecessor without making your team seem bad too. They will not like it. And they won't like you. Avoid this.

Moving too fast.
The risk here is that you'll make poor decisions and come across as too impulsive. So, again, target giving yourself at least 30 days. By the 30-day mark, you will have had a chance to see people in action, and you can now make your decisions based on past performance, feedback from others, and your own observations.

Moving too slow.
As mentioned before, moving too slowly is an even more significant risk. At the 100-day mark, you own the team. Once you're the owner, all the problem kids are yours. You can't blame them on your predecessor any more.

Don't fool yourself. Your team members know who the weak links are. And the number one thing high performers want is for you to act on low performers so the whole group can do better. If you move too slowly, the other team members will wonder what took you so long.

Losing your top performers.
Keeping a cloud of uncertainty about who will (and will not) be on the team can lead your best people to bolt. Although you should be cautious about what you say before your changes are finalized, you should look for ways to signal to your top performers that you recognize their value and consider them keepers. A little reassurance can go a long way toward retaining your top talent.

Don't underestimate the time needed to get everything done.
You may need to put in place transition plans, support weaker

team members or keep strong team members in the wrong roles temporarily while you take time to get their replacements hired and up to speed. So take this into account as you plan the timing of your restructuring. It may take longer than you think.

Trying to do it all by yourself.
Finally, keep in mind that the process of restructuring a team is fraught with emotional, legal, and company policy complications.

Even though you're an HR pro yourself, do *not* try to undertake this on your own. Find out who you can best use as an objective sounding board in charting your strategy. Tapping into another set of HR eyes and getting wise legal counsel is indispensable in restructuring your team.

Summary & Action Steps

Unless you're in a start-up, you typically don't get to build your HR team from scratch. You typically inherit a team that you should be prepared to reshape to deliver your agenda.

The process of molding a team is like changing a flat tire on a car while it's moving. You will not reach your destination if you ignore doing it. But you do not want to crash the car while trying to fix it.

In your case, you need to replace people on the team, but what do you do if they are critical to managing workload in the short run?

The answer is straightforward.

You develop options as quickly as possible and don't delay implementing them. This means making tough decisions around:

1. When to make changes in your team.
2. How to make changes in your team.
3. Avoiding common traps in the process.

At the 30-day point, but certainly no longer than 60 days, you should begin executing your changes. This may mean applying stop-gap measures. Like hiring people into temporary positions. Or testing whether people further down in the organization can stretch up and deliver more.

However, if you wait more than 100 days, the team becomes "yours," and changes made after that can become more difficult to justify and carry out.

* * *

Rule #12:
LEVERAGE THE "F" WORD
FREQUENTLY

As a kid, I remember my mom rubbing antiseptic ointment onto my bloodied knee after falling off my bike.

"It hurts!" I sobbed.

"That means it's working," she said wisely.

Sometimes what's good for you hurts a little too.

And getting brutally candid personal feedback is one of those things. It's that **notorious "F" word** that often stings and can be uncomfortable to hear.

But it's essential to your success.

In fact, "Getting Feedback" is Critical Boss Conversation #6 – first referenced back in Rule #6. And as such, you should proactively solicit it from your boss -- and also from your key clients, within the <u>first 30-60 days</u> in your new HR leadership role.

And then ACT on it.

If you have concerns at all about seeking it out, let me suggest thinking about feedback this way:

- It's a GIFT -- of time, honesty, and thoughtful insight from people with opinions you value.
- It's a GIFT that will help you adjust your leadership style and elevate your performance.
- And, as with any GIFT, the best response to any feedback – good or bad, whether you agree with it or not – is "thank you!"

Now with this in mind, there are **two types of feedback** you specifically want to go after:

Type #1:
Feedback on Your Style and "Fit."

The most crucial early feedback won't pertain to your job performance unless it has been truly awful. Instead, it will relate to the "softer" aspects of your style in leading, working, and communicating with others. This kind of feedback will clue you into early issues with the "fit" of your personal style with the organization's culture, which is crucial.

However, getting specific, actionable feedback from your boss, clients, or colleagues can be tough to obtain -- even if you beg them for it.

And the reason is that many people are uncomfortable providing it.

They'll change the subject if they believe this will start a pissing contest with you.

Or they'll sugarcoat their comments so as to not bruise your feelings.

Or they'll cloak their statements in vague or fuzzy language that leave you uncertain about what they really mean.

On the latter point, here are some vague feedback examples:

> *"You can improve your relationships more..."*
> *"Work on being a little less abrasive..."*
> *"You can be serious at times. Lighten up."*
> *"Some people believe you're not a team player..."*

The problem is that none of these comments are *actionable* -- though all are extremely important for you to know.

So, if you're having trouble decoding what you're hearing, follow up and probe deeper. Ask: "What one or two things – beyond anything else – would you recommend that I do that would help me address this and be more effective?"

From such additional probes, you are looking for responses such as these:

> *"Work on being a bit more positive. For example, you do a fantastic job of identifying issues in our leadership meetings but don't spend enough time bringing solutions to help. Here are two examples..."*

> *"I'd like to see more of a sense of urgency. For example, it takes your team too long to call me back on job offers. I'd like more status updates. On the R&D Director candidate, in particular, you guys..."*

These are good, actionable feedback statements. Anything close to these is exactly what you want and can significantly help clarify puzzling comments.

Don't argue or debate the feedback you're getting. This will help your feedback providers get past their hesitation to be candid.

So stay in active listening mode and **recognize that you don't have to agree with everything.** It's OK to ask clarifying questions but avoid debates. (You can always correct the facts later, but this isn't the time). The worst thing you can say in one of these sessions is: *"I disagree with that,"* or *"Here's why you're wrong..."*

That kind of defensive reaction will shut down the free flow of feedback from them in a New York minute. Or it will steer it to safer (and much vaguer) fuzzy-word territory. None of which will be helpful to you.

Finally, thank your feedback providers and let them know what actions you plan to take based on their feedback. This will help build the relationship and make it more comfortable for them to offer such feedback in the future.

The bottom line is if there are issues with your style, approach, or behavior, be prepared to flex them. This doesn't mean you have to do a personality transplant, but it does mean that you should explore different ways to get things done.

Type #2:
Feedback on Your Pace.

Pace refers to how quickly you're moving and getting important things done. Key questions here include:

- How much time are you devoting to **learning activities** like meetings, connecting with key people, and deepening your understanding of your new organization?

- How much time are you spending on **results-producing activities** such as making key decisions, driving change, recruiting new people, solving client problems, getting alignment to important initiatives, and so on?

In other words, are you striking the **right balance** between these two activities?

There is only ONE answer to this question…

It depends on why you were hired in the first place.

For example, if you're joining a well-functioning HR team already delivering strong results, you may have the luxury of doing more <u>learning</u> early on.

In situations like these, short term, you can do quite well just sustaining the existing success. There may be little need for you to jump into the fray and make lots of early disruptive decisions. Your team may not need significant direction from you initially, and the organization may not be hungry for lots of change driven by HR.

Consequently, you can afford to delve deeply into your learning first and aim carefully before firing your first critical shots. Obviously, the risks in these situations are that any early mistakes on your part, especially if they are interpreted as disrupting a well-oiled machine, can cost you dearly.

So the good news here is that you will have time to place a premium on your learning. However, the downside is such situations rarely last long.

That brings us to the **second scenario.**

This is where you've been brought aboard to:

- **Start up a new HR function from scratch.**
- **Lead a significant HR transformational initiative.**
- **Support a high-growth business or one that is declining.**
- **Fix a poor-performing HR team with little credibility.**

In these cases, <u>execution</u> should be your focus as you may be expected to show results quickly.

If you spend too much time learning, you'll raise questions about your leadership capability, HR competence, and why it's taking you so long to get up to speed and show value.

This is not to say that learning is unimportant in these situations. It just means that you should *accelerate* the process and be prepared to make some early decisions without having 100% full information. Or fire some shots before you are confident of your aim and then adjust quickly if you're off the mark or get push back.

Obviously, this balance between learning and action isn't an exact science.

But it is essential that you know your charter and what kind of situation you're stepping into -- and recognize that organizations change quickly.

This is why setting aside time to get feedback on your pace is crucial. You don't want your movement (too fast or too slow) to be out of step with that of the organizations and your key stakeholders.

Summary & Action Steps

Getting candid feedback can feel as uncomfortable as a kid's bloodied knee. But paraphrasing my mom: sometimes what hurts a bit at first can be good for you in the long run when you take the right action against it.

And that's how feedback should be treated. Getting it early and often is crucial, and the more direct and brutally candid it is, the better. You should solicit it regularly from your boss and clients within your first 30 -60 days.

Specifically, you should go out and ask for two types of feedback:

1. **Feedback on your style, approach, and "fit"**
2. **Feedback on your pace.**

Once you've received it, make adjustments. Consider all feedback – good and bad – a gift. When receiving it, thank the giver.

* * *

Rule #13:
IGNITE THE FIRE
WITHIN YOUR TEAM

The best leaders create engaged, passionate teams. No one enjoys going to work if they're simply going to grind through their day, facing nothing but an endless stream of problems, day in and day out. Most people don't mind challenging work but want to be led by someone who can also provide direction, spark, and inspiration.

And that person should be you.

As the new HR leader, it's up to you to create that positive "buzz" that radiates energy and provides a source of motivation for your team.

However, this takes work, doesn't happen overnight, and takes time to lay the proper foundation. Specifically, it requires that you first:

- Take Charge With Confidence (Rule #4)
- Get On Top of Current Projects (Rule #6)
- Clarify Expectations (Rule #8)
- Cut the Fat and Muscle Up Your Team (Rule #11)

Again, these are the basics -- the key foundations that are your priority. Only AFTER you've completed them have you set the stage for really "lighting a fire" underneath your team and taking things to an entirely new level.

One other point I've said before, but want to make sure you don't miss...

**Igniting your team is especially crucial if
you've <u>cut staff, added new people</u> or
<u>dramatically reorganized</u> your team.**
(More specifically, if you've completed Rule #11).

And, no matter how smoothly you've made these kinds of changes, some members of your team will feel fear, uncertainty, and distrust. They'll have questions about their security and value to you and their future.

Clearly you can't make guarantees and shouldn't betray confidences. But you can't let these negative feelings fester either because they can become cancerous and potentially undermine your efforts.

So, in this situation, rebuilding the team and re-sparking their passion for the challenges ahead is even more critical.

Here are **four essential strategies** for igniting your team:

#1: Step Up Your Level of Passion.

It all starts with YOU.

To ignite the fire within your team, you must first energize yourself. This starts with believing in what you're doing and that the changes you've made are the right ones. And then spreading that conviction to your team. You can't ignite passion with a wet match.

It needs a spark.

And that spark must be you.

Your team is looking to you for inspiration. They see you on your best days as a beacon of hope, enthusiasm, and insight. And they see you on your worst days when you seem distant, cheerless, or disconnected. Unfortunately, when you spend most of your waking hours with people, your best and worst will come to the surface.

So, it's vital that, no matter how you feel, you be perceived as passionate about the organization and ecstatic for your HR team. Once you've made difficult changes, this becomes more important than ever.

#2: Meet Individually To Stabilize And Re-Recruit Your People.

Let them know they're valued.
Meet with each of them individually and stress their importance. They need to look you in the eye and hear directly from you how valued they are to the team, the organization, and to you. Even if you've done this before, repetition doesn't hurt.

Here's why. If you've made massive changes, you must work to restore trust. It is damaged. Whether they are losing a valued colleague you've fired or reshuffling their responsibilities, individuals within your team are experiencing a loss. A loss of the familiar.

People will grieve even if they recognize the changes you've made are good for them and for the team in the long term. You will even have a few people -- the survivors -- who feel guilty that you've chosen to retain them in their roles. *So, it's up to you to recognize all this by connecting with everyone on your team individually. And then give them some time and space to deal with their temporary feelings of anger and loss.*

Re-prioritize the goals and workload.
Change hits people differently. Some members of your team may view the changes you've made as exciting and career-expanding. For others, not so much.

In one reorganization I did, one of my HR managers had to temporarily step in and handle the workload done previously by three others. After suffering in silence for a week, she finally exploded and let me know she felt overworked and under-appreciated. She was absolutely right, and I immediately lightened her load. If this happens to you:

- Look for ways to streamline current work. If you temporarily have fewer people, bring in short-term help or work with your clients to re-prioritize projects and the support you're providing. Solicit ideas from your team on how this can be best done.

- Re-examine the goals and commitments you've set. Make certain your daily tasks are focused, like a laser beam, on your most important deliverables.

Have career talks.
This is also an excellent time for individual discussions with your staff about their future. Identify additional learning, work experiences, and support that will enhance their career opportunities.

Above all, your goal is to help people feel confident that they can contribute, grow further, and feel more comfortable about the changed work environment within the team.

#3: Define A New Uplifting Vision.

With your arrival, your direct reports will expect you to clarify the team's direction and priorities going forward.

Whether you choose to call this a "vision," "mission," or "purpose" or simply a "new direction" is immaterial.

What is important is that as the new HR leader, you take the lead in clarifying the future and where the team is headed.

You can either do this alone or engage your team in the process. I highly recommend doing the latter as an offsite meeting because it will further strengthen buy-in.

Taking your team offsite.
This is an ideal way to re-engage, refresh and re-energize the whole team – while getting their help mapping the future direction and priorities of the group.

Investing a day or two away from the daily tasks and spending time together can have a tremendous payoff in the team's long-term enthusiasm and vitality.

Be clear about your offsite goals, and create an agenda that re-inforces those goals. Make sure that everyone knows that the offsite should be a safe space where people can speak up and constructively challenge one another -- and even you, without any fear of reprisal.

It's also helpful to pledge confidentiality, meaning that the content of what is said at the offsite is for you and your team alone and will not get communicated to others back at the office — unless the group agrees to authorize specific messages or information that will be shared.

Focus on doing real work. For example, in looking at all the demands facing the team, your team may want to consider the following options:

Option 1: Revisit the team's direction and game plan the work that needs to be accomplished.
Agenda:
- What's the vision/mission for our team? How do we want to be seen by our key clients?
- Where are our 4-5 most important "A" priorities in the year ahead?
- What hurdles or obstacles do we anticipate encountering in delivering against them?
- How can we address those hurdles?
- What additional help is needed within or outside of the team to help us accomplish this?

Option 2: Create a strategic plan for the future.
Agenda:
- To take our success as a team to the next level -- what 4-5 additional or new HR opportunities should the team tackle? What's the value of these new opportunities to the business?
- What are the resources needed to executive them?
- What additional steps do we need to get these initiatives launched?
- How should accountabilities within the team be divided to get these done?

However, going offsite doesn't have to be focused only on tasks, priorities, and work. In fact, if it's a full day or multi-day offsite, all work and no fun can make for a dull, uninspired session.

Do incorporate fun activities that <u>build the team.</u>
Unfortunately, many offsites that include "fun" or "team building activities" can backfire. Sometimes, it's because the sense of unity and cohesion created when everyone is together having fun outside of the office doesn't last long once everyone gets back home.

Other times, the kinds of team-building activities chosen have the unintended consequence of bringing out competition and hostility instead of enhancing commitment and cohesion within the team.

Along these lines, here's what NOT to do:

- Don't have people dress up in military attire and hunt each other down in the forest, in the jungle, or anywhere else.

- Don't get into go-karts, and try to run each other off the track. Don't do anything else that causes the team to engage in dysfunctional conflict or competition among individuals. Doing so will create dynamics that are "all against all" instead of the desired "all for one and one for all."

- Don't force anyone to sing, dance, listen to karaoke, or participate in "trust falls." Trust falls can end badly, and very few people, unless they're talented, *want* to embarrass themselves by showing why they're not professional entertainers.

These kinds of activities do nothing but breed cynicism and can be viewed as time-wasters by team members.

Ok then, what should you do?
Good question.

One activity that I've found that genuinely builds a sense of teamwork and collaboration is simply cooking a meal together and eating it together as a group. We are a species who bonds over the act of eating. This has been true for hundreds of years. Today, with your team, it's probably no different. There's something about everyone pitching in at mealtime to prepare food, cook it, and dine together that brings people closer together. For more information, google "culinary team building," and you'll find plenty of local restaurants or team building organizations that will set up, manage and run a terrific event for your team.

Another team activity that works well is public service and volunteer projects, such as fixing up a school or playground or building housing for those in need. These can also rebuild team spirit, making every team member feel good about themselves while giving back to the community. If this sounds of interest, reach out to your own in-house public relations group or directly contact local community service organizations to identify opportunities in your area.

However, if none of these ideas work for you, ask your team. Gathering input and suggestions from them can yield better choices for everyone.

If trust is still an issue, gather the input anonymously by hiring an outside facilitator. They can be extremely helpful in interviewing team members and gathering their feedback and suggestions for the planned offsite's structure, fun, and content.

Do build in time to assess and reflect.
Toward the end of the offsite meeting, ask yourself and your team:

- How did we do in achieving our goals for this meeting?
- How did we do as a team in terms of creating more effective patterns for communication and collaboration -- or of discussion and debate?
- How effective was my leadership of this meeting? What worked well? What should I do differently?
- When we return to work, what should we carry from this meeting into our day-to-day work as a team?
- What 1-2 messages or key talking points should we convey to others if asked about our offsite?

Do schedule follow-ups.
The most common complaint about a team building offsite is that there is either insufficient or no follow-up. When that happens, any progress made turns out to be temporary, and any goals set tend to fall by the wayside.

Scheduling a follow-up offsite, or at least check-in meetings, at the three-month point, six-month points, and a year after the initial offsite can help ensure that the team stays focused on making progress and sustaining positive change.

A successful team building offsite can enable the team to change old patterns, re-commit and create new ways of communicating and collaborating, thereby changing the team's dynamics for the better.

#4: Create Defining Moments.

One of the best strategies for re-energizing your team is to **look for or create moments to acknowledge your team's efforts and results.** Here are a few suggestions:

Recognize victories.

Acknowledging your team members for their excellent work and effort goes a long way. It doesn't matter if it's done publicly or privately. Just do it.

How do you approach this? It's simple. Go on the hunt for victories: clients delighted, problems solved, mistakes avoided, and metrics exceeded. Brains like victories. So call attention to the victors. Celebrate them. Engineer some victories to celebrate. Find real reasons for the people on your team to feel successful.

For example, if you have just joined a team that is wrapping up a successful year of MBA recruiting, let everyone enjoy the thank you's. Even if you weren't around for the whole year, step back and let everyone walk around with the trophy. Take everyone out to lunch. Let everyone laugh. Let others glow in the feeling of accomplishing a mutual goal. Show your enthusiasm for their win.

Some companies have formal methods for recognition, such as award nominations or emailed forms of appreciation. Use these company-recognized tools to the max. Also, use informal methods such as giving shoutouts during a team meeting, just sending an informal email -- or craft an old-school handwritten thank-you note. In fact, you may want to buy a box of thank you notes just for this purpose.

Champion your people to your boss.
Bring them to important meetings, showcasing them where appropriate. Allow your people to present their accomplishments to the higher-ups.

This is a great way to re-engage your team and shows them (and your boss) what kind of leader you are. However, make sure you prep them in advance and debrief together afterward. An essential part of your job is to shine a spotlight on the good works of your team.

Provide opportunities to develop and stretch.
If you aren't creating these kinds of opportunities, you are not only doing a disservice to your people, you are harming yourself. The success of a leader is the success of the team. There is no more tremendous success than developing your team members.

Stretch assignments are also an excellent tool when thinking about their career paths. For example, if your team member has defined their desired next step, find stretch assignments that let them improve their knowledge and relationships.

Be there to support and offer guidance but remember to let them have time to experience and ultimately succeed.

Typically, after someone has been in a position for about two years, it is time to examine their next steps. That's not to say someone can't promote after six months or stay in the same job for five years, but consider what can happen in two years. The first year is a learning and growth year. In the second year, they'll begin to perfect their work and stretch into more responsibilities. Then, when they've had that stellar second or third year, be ready to support their next step.

Simply show you care.
The little things count, sustain people through tough times, and show you care. Below are some ways of demonstrating this. I'm

not saying do these every day or even once a week. But on occasion, consider the following:

- **Remember birthdays and anniversaries.** Put these on your calendar with a reminder a few days in advance. Bring the donuts, bagels, or fruit and circulate the greeting card. *Model what other leaders do in your company.* At PepsiCo, we printed birthday signs, decorated cubicles, and brought a cake into a conference room. To some, these actions may seem a bit childish, but everyone likes to have a day dedicated to them.

- **Buy breakfast for absolutely no reason.** Sometimes, even when it's not someone's birthday, pick up something for breakfast for the team. Maybe a new bakery just opened by the office, or you happen to be running early on the way to work. Grab a box of donuts, breakfast sandwiches, or a fruit tray. It doesn't matter what, just bring in something to show you appreciate that people chose to wake up that morning and came in to spend it working with you.

- **Have team lunches.** Team lunches strengthen relationships through conversation and interaction. People are generally relaxed when eating and far more willing to share. New ideas can be discussed and grown into new strategies. A tense mood can be lightened. Stories can be shared that deepen personal and professional relationships. You can do this randomly and without planning, now and then.

  However, remember that some on diets bring their own lunch, and some may run errands or visit the gym. And still others use this time to get work done. So don't assume that everyone will always be available to dine with you on a whim.

- **Connect the dots for your team.** At the end of 60 days, you should know how your team's work contributes to the organization's larger goal. Share these and other insights with your team. Help them connect the dots.

Regularly explain what your team does that benefits the company. If the team didn't exist, what might happen?

Failing to both *see* and *feel* their connection to the organization's larger vision is one of the main reasons your people will leave -- especially your high-potential talent. So regularly talk through the importance of the work they do.

Here's the bottom line on all this. **People don't care how much you know until they know how much you care.** So, don't hesitate to show appreciation to your team as individuals, not just contributors. Learn something new each day about one of them. Ask them about their families, hobbies, and leisure activities. Then weave this information into your interactions with them. They will return your appreciation and attention with inspired performance.

Summary & Action Steps

The best HR leaders can create energized, passionate teams. As a new HR leader, you want to create a culture that ignites your team and makes people enjoy coming to work. You are ready to ignite your team of direct reports once you've completed the following:

- Taken charge with confidence (Rule #4)
- Gotten on top of current projects (Rule #6)
- Clarified expectations (Rule #8)
- Cut the fat and muscled up your team (Rule #11)

However, igniting (re-igniting) your team is especially crucial immediately after you've *cut staff, added new people,* or *dramatically reorganized* your team. To accomplish this requires that you execute the following:

1. Step up your own level of passion.
2. Meet one-on-one to stabilize and re-recruit your people.

3. Define a new uplifting vision.
4. Create defining moments.

Finally, building a passionate, productive, and committed team requires attention to the little things that will inspire them and show you care.

* * *

Rule #14:
SCORE SMART EARLY WINS
TO MAKE YOUR MARK

Before your 100 days end, if you haven't already, you need to score some wins. Unfortunately, new HR leaders have a short grace period in today's impatient, results-now world.

So, it's entirely natural for you to want to act quickly and do something dramatic. You may be itching to put some points on the board fast to prove to your organization that you're the brilliant, savvy HR leader they're hoping they've hired.

And that is absolutely the correct instinct.

However, slow down just a second, tiger. As important as wins are, it's essential that you pick the right ones -- the **smart** wins.

With that in mind, here are **ten guidelines** for selecting and posting smart early wins:

#1: Know What A "Win" Really Is.

This can vary widely from one organization to another. For example, in some organizations, a win has to be a visible individual achievement. In others, accomplishing results solo without engaging others, even if they deliver fantastic results, can backfire and label you as a glory hound and anti-team.

Similarly, if you work in an organization that values teamwork and collaboration, smart early wins could come in the form of leading a team in solving a long-standing problem like retaining top talent, improving employee engagement or reducing overhead costs…or being viewed as a solid team player and key contributor to such initiatives. However, in another organization, doing this same thing might be viewed as just another ho-hum activity if it fails to produce visible or quantifiable results.

The point: be sure you understand what your organization *does* and *does not* view as a win.

#2: Identify A Short List Of 3-5 Potential Smart Win Candidates -- Then Select Two From Your List.

One or two smart wins are about all you can handle well in your first 100 days. The ones you choose should address the most prominent "pain points" you've heard from your clients.

For example, from the list below, what are the 1-2 most important results your clients are counting on you and your team to deliver quickly?

- Is it improving the retention of their top talent?
- Is it driving cost savings or helping them cut overhead?
- Is it acquiring more or higher quality job candidates?
- Is it improving morale in the customer service group?
- Is it improving the results from the sales force?
- Is it upgrading the leadership talent in some regions?
- Is it executing against their talent strategy faster?
- Is it improving teamwork within their business?
- Is it bringing in cost-effective new HR best practices?
- Is it expanding the online presence of the company?
- Is it reducing overtime, tardiness or sick leave usage?

Start with questions like these and choose your targets well. Then, pick opportunities that you're sure you and your team can deliver on that play to your team's strengths, and that would not have happened if you had not been there.

Here are a couple of examples:

Example 1: Let's say the company is trying to improve its online sales of new products. And you understand that one of your key clients, the Marketing group, is struggling to come up with fresh, innovative ideas needed to capitalize on social media.

This is your cue to jump into the mix. You could work with them to attract new innovative marketing talent savvy in social media. If you can bring in 2-3 new people to the team in ten days with the desired skills they need – and source these hires in a way they absolutely could not have done without your assistance – this could represent a tremendous early win.

Example 2: Imagine you're in a big meeting about cutting costs. If you're able to chime in with a perspective on the high costs of current incentive pay plans (if your expertise is total rewards) or the company's high price tag in subcontracting out union work (if labor relations is your area of specialty), then you instantly can become a significant player in these discussions.

And more importantly, if you can then volunteer your HR team to lead a key cost-reduction initiative in these or related areas, this could be the starting point for an excellent early and smart win.

You want to find problems plaguing the business that you can fix with HR solutions. Then fix them. **It doesn't matter how big or small they are because your short-term goal is to build a reputation as someone who gets things done in areas that the business values.**

#3: Make Sure the Wins You Choose Matter To Your Boss.

Ideally, if your boss can hand you some early win projects that hit their hot buttons, that's terrific. If not, identify them yourself (see #2 above).

If you've selected them yourself, weigh your boss's opinion and priorities heavily before you finalize your choice. Addressing problems that your boss cares about will go a long way toward building your credibility.

#4: Ensure The Result Is Clearly Measurable.

The last thing you want is a performance review with your boss after all the hours you put into your project -- and suddenly, you cannot assess whether your early win was a success. Right? Right.

This is why the result should be clear and measurable. You're in great shape if you can measure your success using the financials or analytics widely embraced within the organization (e.g. costs, SG&A, turnover, productivity, engagement metrics, etc.).

Here's how to approach measuring your results: (1) Pick an issue or project you're trying to address (ex: retaining high-producing salespeople), (2) Put a metric to it, and (3) When you've improved that metric, you've added value, and that becomes the measure of your success. Don't over-complicate this.

#5: Pick Wins As Early As You Can. Focus on Those Achievable Within Your First 3-6 Months.

These will give your boss talking points when someone asks how you are doing. But, again, these shouldn't be huge, game-changing initiatives that take two years to accomplish. Those are important for you to work on but aren't what you're looking for as your smart early wins. While you want to deliver early successes, you don't want them to take forever to achieve.

#6: A Win Should Be "Owned" By You.

This means you need to be able to attach your name to it. This can be tricky. It doesn't mean you swoop in to take sole credit for a team win…don't do that!

Let them take the bows, but make sure this is something you are instrumental in leading and helping to achieve.

#7: Don't Bite Off More Than You Can Chew.

Again, select no more than one or two important early wins to go after. It is easy to tackle too much during your first 100 days, and the results can be disastrous.

Therefore, it is essential to identify promising opportunities and focus relentlessly on translating them into wins. Then, put more resources than you think you could justify against these early opportunities so you and your team can deliver them better and faster than anyone could have ever thought possible.

#8: Pre-Wire Wins If You Anticipate Huge Resistance.

Let's say your boss has asked you to lead the implementation of a significant HR strategic initiative -- for example, driving big improvements in the performance review system or executing substantial changes in the bonus program for the national sales force.

Even if the need for change in these areas is well-recognized, you're likely to face pushback when the time comes to implement the new program or solution. And you should anticipate this. In such situations, you'll want to pre-wire first.

Pre-wiring is the old concept of taking the key stakeholders or decision-makers through the key elements of your execution plan early. This is to obtain and incorporate their input <u>long before</u> actual execution happens or before seeking their final approval. Pre-wiring ensures that their fingerprints are all over what you plan to do and that there are no shocking revelations or surprises for them when the time comes for you to take action.

If you shortcut and neglect doing this, you should expect key decision-makers to resist strongly, complain loudly, and treat you as if you're a convicted serial killer – all to protect themselves from something they aren't ready for.

Don't allow this to happen.

To effectively pre-wire, send out a summary of your draft plan before you seek final buy-in and request lots of feedback and comments. Or even better yet, schedule some in-depth one-on-ones with a few of the key influencers beforehand. Taking the time to do any of this will dramatically elevate your chances for success.

#9: "How" You Get The Win Matters.

This was touched on earlier, but let me drive the message home even more clearly. *If you deliver excellent results in a manner seen as manipulative, underhanded, or inconsistent with the culture, that's not a win. It's a loss. And can be tough to recover from.* So plan to deliver your win in a way that exhibits the types of leadership behaviors that the organization values.

#10: Finally, DO Publicize Your Wins.

Strong HR leaders also are not hesitant to publicize their winning results. This is essential in making your mark. However, they do it subtly, in a way that won't alienate others or label them as egotistical jerks in the minds of their colleagues.

There are a variety of ways of accomplishing this. For example, with a win under your belt, you can **offer to share your results and experiences** in HR-related lunch and learn sessions, training programs, at quarterly meetings -- or better yet, farm yourself out to other divisions/groups within your organization as a resource in **solving similar kinds of problems.**

If your actions are geared solely toward benefiting others, your reputation and credibility will grow and spread quickly throughout the organization.

Summary & Action Steps

Selecting early wins is important. Tangible results, delivered fast, is the best way to validate the decision to place you in your new HR leadership role. But you must choose **smart,** early wins.

To this end, make a conscious decision to **identify 1-2 wins** you'll go after -- and use the following **ten guidelines** described in this chapter to guide you in selecting and executing them successfully:

1. Know what a "win" really is.
2. Identify a short list of 3-5 potential smart win candidates and then select two from your list.
3. Make sure the wins you choose matter to your boss.
4. Ensure the result is clearly measurable.
5. Pick wins as early as you can. Focus on those achievable within your first 3-6 months.
6. A win should be "owned" by you.
7. Don't bite off more than you can chew.
8. Pre-wire wins if you anticipate massive resistance.
9. "How" you get the win matters.
10. Finally, do publicize your wins.

* * *

Rule #15:
TRACK YOUR ACCOMPLISHMENTS

This is the final rule, and it may well be the most important.

Whether your review is done <u>formally</u> or <u>informally</u> -- quarterly, at midyear, annually -- or <u>not at all</u> -- tracking your accomplishments is an absolute MUST DO!

Let me be even blunter about this point.

Some organizations consider your first 100-days, NOT your honeymoon period, BUT your *probationary period* – whether they state this explicitly or not. And as such, some have the patience of a gnat with new HR leaders...and won't hesitate to cut bait at the drop of a hat -- especially if the business is tanking and you're not delivering. You know it, and I know it.

Further, if you do make it to your first performance review, we both know that reviews aren't always as objective as they should be. It's easy for an overworked boss to forget how excited she was about that great new talent retention initiative you spearheaded in February – if your review is not until November. Therefore, you should help your boss (and yourself) by regularly documenting what you have accomplished.

Waiting until a few days before a review session is too late. You'll forget significant results and details.

The point: Keep a record of your achievements as they occur, so you can provide your own fact-based, detailed input or self-assessment when review time comes.

To accomplish this, there are **four steps** to follow:

Step #1:
Create a Capturing Mechanism.

This can be as simple as creating a special folder on your laptop. This will ensure you've consolidated all your accomplishments in one spot.

Label it "My Performance Results" or "My Accomplishments." Use it to save all the e-mail feedback, electronic compliments, and kudos you receive from clients, peers, and managers throughout the year — including your boss, their boss, and all other leaders between you and the CEO.

Step #2:
Start Capturing
Your Accomplishments.

Include the following in this folder regularly (for example, every Friday afternoon):

- Progress against the performance expectations you and your boss agreed on (see Rule #8).
- New problems you solved or solutions you introduced.
- Key projects, metrics, and performance standards you completed or exceeded.
- Other unplanned significant accomplishments.

This includes even more detailed personal notes to yourself. Do this by asking: *"In what areas have I been able to:*

- Accomplish more with the same
- Accomplish the same thing with less
- Create something from scratch
- Develop a new process
- Do what couldn't be done
- Enhance the impact of an HR initiative
- Expand the reach of an HR initiative

- Establish a new process, system, or procedure
- Find a better strategy or alternative
- Find a cheaper solution
- Find a new opportunity
- Find an easier solution
- Foresee a need
- Foresee a problem
- Foresee an opportunity
- Improve client relations
- Improve client satisfaction
- Improve employee relations
- Improve labor/management relations
- Improve quality
- Improve teamwork
- Increase ROI
- Make fewer bad things happen
- Make more good things happen
- Make things easier
- Make things smoother
- Overcome obstacles
- Prevent a problem
- Provide new resources
- Receive an award
- Reduce costs
- Reduce errors
- Reduce losses
- Save the day
- Solve a chronic problem
- Speed things up

Step #3:
Do Your Own "Self-Appraisals" Each Month.

Use the information you've captured to conduct your own monthly mini-reviews informally. Do this well before you meet with your manager. Be honest with yourself — evaluate your progress against your boss' expectations or performance objectives. Then, summarize what you've accomplished and rate yourself each month.

Be objective and evaluate the dents and dings in your performance too. That is, dust-ups you've had with your boss or clients, missed deadlines, and situations where you were just off your game. Of course, you want to avoid surprise hits and anticipate answers in advance, if you need to explain your shortfalls. The beauty of monthly self-appraisals is that they give you time to make mid-course corrections if you feel you are getting off track.

And doing them consistently should inoculate you against shocks and surprises when *real* appraisal time arrives.

Step #4:
Focus on Quantifying
Your Contributions.

As you should know by now, I'm a maniac for numbers especially for HR leaders. Numbers are the language of business. But, also, there is a more subtle reason. Optically, the human eye gravitates to quantifiable symbols (e.g., $, #, or %). You should leverage this fact when the time comes to capture your accomplishments and provide input for your final review.

So when you list your achievements, focus on the quantifiable impact on the business. Examples:

- Did you oversee negotiating a new union labor contract __% below your company's approved budgeted costs?
- Did you spearhead the reduction in the cost of turnover in the customer service group by $____ due to the new job rotation program you put in place for customer care specialists?
- Did you architect a new, out-of-the-box approach to talent acquisition that dramatically improved cost-per-hire by $___ and enhanced quality-of-hire by ___%?

So, wherever you can, quantification is the winning ticket to clarifying and adding power to your accomplishments rather than using words alone.

Remember, following these four steps isn't mandatory. But it is an opportunity for you to inform your manager about the performance results you achieved, the challenges you faced, and the learning and development you desire.

Summary & Action Steps

During your first 100 days, you should begin tracking your accomplishments to prepare for your inevitable performance review – if and when it occurs. To get ahead of the game, you should:

1. Create a capturing mechanism.
2. Start capturing your accomplishments in it.
3. Do your own self-appraisals each month.
4. Focus on quantifying your contributions.

You can't rely on your boss to stay on top of your performance. So this falls on you to take charge of the process.

* * *

Bonus Rule #16:
ACT QUICKLY ON WARNING SIGNS THAT YOUR NEW JOB MAY BE IN JEOPARDY

Hopefully, you've reviewed the first 15 rules and are excited about putting them into action.

However, my goal is to over-deliver in this book and ensure you get as much value as possible. So I've included two extra bonus rules – #16 and 17.

In this particular rule, I want to prepare you to act on cues that your new position might be at risk.

Here's the deal: no one is immune from getting downsized, laid off, or fired. Clearly, the stronger you're performing, the smaller the chance of that happening. But don't let this fact prevent you from acting on the tell-tale signals.

What makes all this especially difficult is that it's likely you WON'T be warned or know in advance that you're about to get canned. Even if you're the HR lead in charge of all organization-wide layoffs yourself, you won't find out if you've been terminated until it happens! With this in mind, here are **ten warning signs** to be aware of and how to address them.

Warning Sign #1:
You Have a Brand New Boss
With A Mandate For Change.

When Marissa Mayer joined Yahoo as CEO years ago, she immediately did something typical. She shook up the HR group.

She immediately replaced Yahoo's long-time SVP of HR and his number two executive, the VP of talent acquisition.

According to insiders, these moves surprised no one since Mayer came into a poorly-performing organization with a clear charter from the Board to turn around the business. Upon her arrival, she aggressively took control of Yahoo's culture and HR, which included installing Google-style talent practices, doing things the "Google Way," and making Yahoo a smaller version of Google, a firm Mayer had worked for her entire career.

This kind of house cleaning should be anticipated when a new leader lands on the premises with a mandate for change. Like a new football coach hired to take a losing team to the Super Bowl, you should expect actions to wake up the talent, trim the fat, or install their own team -- just as you did when you assumed your new HR role.

Here's the point: When a new boss arrives, no matter how well you've been doing, it's like starting a new job. You have to prove yourself all over again. That boss will judge your performance against new criteria — their metrics and not your old boss's. And if the new boss hints about a great friend they've worked with who has held your position, that's a surefire sign they may have designs on your job.

What to do: Many HR leaders make the mistake of continuing to work as they did before the new boss arrived, thinking that the boss has to get acclimated to the culture, not them. But that's a prescription for getting a surprise heave-ho.

The new boss has a mandate, and you need to understand what it is and that you're fully and completely aligned with it. If you're not, you're toast.

Warning Sign #2:
Your Employer's Financial
Results Suck.

If your organization is not making money or meeting the business plan, it's ripe for change, whether it is job cuts, a reorganization, or pursuing a new business strategy. Either way, as a newcomer, you have to realize you may be a prime candidate for termination.

What to do: Brutally assess how HR is viewed inside your organization. If it's regarded unfavorably by the higher-ups, expect drastic changes. The CEO and the key business leaders might make cuts, outsource significant portions of HR work or eliminate some HR leaders to reduce costs. All of these actions are ridiculously short-sighted, but they have become routine. Because of this, consider poor financial results for 2-3 quarters in a row a cue for you to start exploring other job opportunities.

Warning Sign #3:
Your Company Has Been Sold, Merged, Or Taken Over.

If your company or your division is sold, realize that there will be redundant positions, and your job could be affected -- no matter at what level in the organization you currently reside.

What to do: Having personally survived the merger between Quaker Oats and PepsiCo, here's my best advice: Always have a polished power point deck ready that shows the value you are providing to the firm so that when your company is taken over, you can use it as your sales pitch to the new CHRO or your new boss. Also, don't wait for a meeting to be scheduled by the new leadership to make your case. Instead, take the bull by the horns and be ready to make a positive first impression proactively.

Warning Sign #4:
You're Out of the Loop.

As an HR leader, your insights, perspectives, and points of view make you valuable. Consequently, if you're excluded from key meetings, not ever asked to weigh in on HR strategies, staffing decisions, or key talent initiatives, it signals several things: (a) that your boss, colleagues, or clients don't view you as strategic, (b) your boss has lost (or never had) confidence in you, or (c) you're viewed as an impediment to getting things done, and they'd sooner move on without you.

These are all signs that you're no longer in the loop and your expertise is not valued. And it might only be a matter of time before you're shown the door.

What to do: Get feedback from your boss, clients, and colleagues on why your insights are not fully tapped or utilized. Listen carefully to their responses. Then, take any corrective actions suggested. Keep soliciting feedback to assess your progress. At the same time, polish up your resume, start returning recruiters' phone calls, and reactivate your network, just in case.

Warning Sign #5:
Your Boss's Behavior Towards You Has Dramatically Changed.

If they are increasingly unavailable to you, cancel routine meetings, and seem to be spending more time behind closed doors...all these are clear indications that you and your boss are drifting apart. Unless you get back in alignment, your job may be at risk.

What to do: Find out from your boss why communications seem to be drying up. Clearly, you're not the priority you once were. Otherwise, they'd devote more time to you. Request candid feedback about how you're doing. Check the rumor mill. Stay persistent. Keep trying to connect with your boss by checking in regularly to ensure you're on the same page.

Warning Sign #6:
You're On Bad Terms With Revenue-Producing Clients.

If the VP of sales starts squawking to the CEO that the new HR guidelines you've implemented prevent her from booking sales, you should be concerned. The last thing you want to do is to be viewed as an HR speed bump that prevents your company from making money.

What to do: Talk to the VP of sales. Determine what her issue is. Get your boss involved if needed. Then fix the problem. ASAP.

Warning Sign #7.
You're Not Getting Buy-In.

Not getting approval for your HR strategy, key talent initiatives, or budget may indicate that the leadership team doesn't support you. It may also suggest that your proposals are not aligned with the business.

Either way, it shows you're not in tune with your colleagues or your organization's needs. And you can't be effective or successful without buy-in.

What to do: Talk with the key decision-makers not giving you the support you need. You might say something like, "I'm sensing an issue around buy-in. On the last two HR projects, I got support from finance and marketing but not from you. Can I get some further insight from you about this? Do you think we're making investments in the right areas?"

In so doing, you show you know what's happening and that you care about their opinion. However, be ready for direct, perhaps uncomfortable feedback.

Warning Sign #8:
You've Engaged in an Unethical,
Illegal or Immoral Activity.

This one is obvious. If you're taking kickbacks from an HR vendor, lying to your boss about your work, guilty of sexual harassment, or fudging your expense book...eventually, you'll get caught and get the boot. And rightly so.

What to do: You're a scumbag, so stop immediately. Re-read your company's policies on ethical behavior. Think about what you're doing and if you'd want to read about it in the local news the next day. Then get ready to pack your stuff. The clock is ticking. It could only be a matter of time.

Warning Sign #9:
The Scope of Your Job
Has Been Reduced.

In your first few months, if your job scope and accountabilities get cut as part of a major HR restructuring, there's a reason. And it's probably because people didn't feel you were up to the task, regardless of what your boss has told you. And that could be a sign that you could be getting moved out soon.

Be skeptical if your boss tells you they are reassigning some of your responsibilities to someone else to lighten your heavy load. It could be just a diplomatic way to say they no longer believe you can do the job.

What to do: Stay positive and assess whether you want to remain in this reduced role. Have a candid discussion with your boss, get advice from your mentors, and tap into the grapevine. In the meantime, do your best in your shrunken capacity while you decide whether to explore the HR job marketplace.

Warning Sign #10:
You Are Re-Assigned To An
Organization-Wide "Special Project."

This could be a good or bad move. Some special project assignments will give you tremendous visibility and act as a career springboard. Other projects are used as an opportunity to free up your current role so that someone else with higher potential can fill it. And then, once the special project role you've filled is completed, that position is eliminated -- and so are you.

What to do: You need to assess the real value of the project on your career. Have a candid discussion with your boss, your mentor, and tap into the grapevine. If the project lacks impact, strong support from the top, or is mere "busywork" -- and your boss pressures you to accept it, it may be too late. The best you can do is keep smiling and take on this new role while dusting off your resume.

Summary & Action Steps

Be aware of **ten tell-tale signs** that your current role may be at risk. They include the following:

1. You have a brand new boss with a mandate for change.
2. Your employer's financial results suck.
3. Your company has been sold, merged, or taken over.
4. You're out of the loop.
5. Your boss' behavior towards you has dramatically changed.
6. You're on bad terms with revenue-producing clients.
7. You're not getting buy-in.
8. You've engaged in an unethical, illegal, or immoral activity.
9. Your job scope has been reduced.
10. You are re-assigned to an organization-wide "special project."

Recognize that no matter your position in HR, especially during the first few months of your tenure, you should have your antennae out for these signals. Recognize them early to take charge and control the actions that will best benefit you and your career.

* * *

Bonus Rule #17:
STAY CURRENT, CAPABLE
AND CHARGED UP

We're now closing in on the end of this book. But, before we part company, I want to leave you with **three final words of wisdom** as part of this bonus rule. Admittedly, there's nothing new or magic here. They are simply common sense nuggets that are easily forgotten as you move forward in your new HR leadership role.

With that in mind, my thoughts…

First of All, Take Care Of Your Health.

This is easy to neglect as an HR leader trying to make your mark. Eighty-hour work weeks. Late-night phone calls. Early morning leadership team meetings. Drinking tons of coffee and eating fast food on the run can all take their toll.

I don't care what kind of shape you are in. You need to schedule time at least three times a week to engage in some physical activity.

What does this have to do with being an effective HR leader? In a word, everything!

Physical exercise of any kind whatsoever, followed by relaxation, will clear your mind and dramatically improve your energy and productivity.

It's a fact.

You are attaching an anchor to your chances of success if you don't care about your health.

Further, abusing your body by smoking, excessive drinking, compulsive eating, and sitting for too long—all add up over time. And they are as bad for your career as neglecting to build your HR competencies, leadership capability, and experiences.

I re-learned this lesson when I started going to the gym again and immediately got re-energized. Even though I knew better, I had gotten woefully out of shape. I had become overwhelmed by my HR work schedule and convinced myself I didn't have time to fit in a daily workout. It was total BS.

You and I know working out and eating healthy is a blinding flash of the obvious. However, even though they know better, many HR leaders treat exercise like a choice.

It's not.

It's now an essential part of performing well and building a successful career in HR.

Jogging. Tennis. Biking. Lifting weights. Tread milling. Doing Pilates.

It's proven. Regular exercise changes your life and makes you more successful.

And frankly, it will also allow you to attract more eyeballs at the beach and fit into your skinny jeans. And that's not such a bad thing, either.

So get up earlier. Turn off the tube. Switch off your little handheld text machine. And sweat. Regularly. Without fail. At least 30 minutes each day.

Because it's worth it.

Secondly, Invest Time in Your Family and "Leave Your Crown in the Garage."

When my son unexpectedly died in an auto accident in 2006, my family was there to help me get through the most emotionally painful ordeal I've ever experienced.

My family was also there on those frequent occasions when I got passed over for HR promotions, yelled at by my boss -- or made stupid mistakes on the job. They were NOT there to provide career advice, but to hear me vent and provide emotional support — which was and is just as important.

Speaking of your family's importance reminds me of a story by Indra Nooyi, who started as CEO during my tenure at Pepsi-Co. Here's Indra describing what happened a few months before my arrival when she was first promoted to President:

I'll never forget coming home after being promoted to Pep-siCo's #2 job in 2001.

My mother was visiting at the time.

"'I've got great news for you," I shouted.

She replied, "It can wait. We need you to go out and get some milk."

"So I go out and get milk. And when I come back, I'm hopping mad. I say: 'I have great news for you. I've just been named President of PepsiCo. And all you want me to do is go out and get milk.'"

Then she says, "Let me explain something to you. You may be President of PepsiCo. But when you step into this house, you're a wife and mother first. Nobody can take that place."

"So leave that crown in the garage!'"

Indra often shares this as one of the most important leadership lessons she's learned after over a decade at the helm of a $166 billion global company.

"No matter who we are or what we do, nobody can take our place in our families."

This theme applies to you as well as an HR leader. Your family and the people you love are essential to your success in HR. Spending time away from them is the price we pay for the long grueling hours trying to get ahead in our careers. Sadly, I know very few people in HR that get this balance right. And I include myself in that group.

However, right now is the best time to contract with yourself to spend more quality alone time with the people most important in your life. Be more available. Listen to and support them more individually. Schedule more social and fun events to enjoy them more. Block time on your calendar. Make it a priority. Yes, even during your first 100 days. You don't want to look back this time next year and say you took them for granted.

If this doesn't seem pressing to you now, know that it will be one day when they're gone, and you realize you didn't show them how much you loved and cherished them.

So go ahead and start planning to do this immediately.

It's not too late.

Finally, Stay Motivated and Inspired.

I know I've alluded to this several times. I will mention it again, this time differently. As an HR leader, you have tremendous power. *You help organizations get better results through people. You help people get better results from their careers.* That's why you get paid. It's a noble calling.

Let this inspire you. Embrace this larger purpose that HR serves. Stick your chest out and wear this badge proudly. As an HR leader, make it your goal to look for opportunities to be a role model and help others individually as an HR pro.

How can you do this?

Well, every single day when you wake up, ask yourself: How can I change someone's life or career today for the better? Then make it your goal to impact <u>one</u> <u>person</u> <u>at</u> <u>a</u> <u>time.</u>

That could include:

- Mentoring up-and-coming high-potentials with bright futures who could profit from your experience.
- Letting a high school student or a college intern "shadow" you for a day to observe you on the job.
- Introducing and connecting people in your network together.
- Volunteering for task force assignments in your company.
- Just showing everyday kindness.

The thrill of helping others succeed can keep your spirits up and keep you inspired.

Also, keep yourself sharp by relentlessly looking for ways to grow your HR competencies and keep your leadership skills up to date. This could include:

- Attending seminars, webinars, conferences, and workshops.
- Visiting other organizations to benchmark best practices.
- Accepting leadership assignments that stretch you.
- Getting coaching from experts and thought leaders.
- Continuing to refine your leadership impact by soliciting regular feedback.
- Embracing HR technology innovations, new metrics, and staying on the leading edge of our profession.

Don't become a dinosaur -- you know what happened to them.

Summary & Action Steps

Make specific plans to stay capable, current, and charged up. This will give you energy, raise your productivity during your first 100 days, and help you sustain it in the months and years ahead. This includes:

1. **Taking care of your health.**
2. **Investing time in your family.**
3. **Staying motivated and inspired.**

Left unaddressed, any of these can turn your new HR role into a nightmare. You reached this point to have a better and happier life.

But you must step away occasionally, trust your team, and find time for yourself. Yes, even during your first 100 days -- and especially in the months beyond this period.

* * *

Final Thoughts

One of these days, you'll transition into a new HR leadership role and want some proven guidance on how to start strong, hit the ground running fast, take charge with confidence and accelerate your success.

You now have it.

If you follow <u>just half</u> of these suggestions in this book, you will have launched yourself well and established a strong foundation for your first 100 days.

Cherish this book and its insights.

Keep it handy for your use in the future.

Or better yet, share it with a colleague or one of your direct reports.

I'm sure they'll appreciate the help.

As I mentioned at the outset, transitioning into a <u>new</u> HR leadership role is the #1 challenge any HR professional can face....no matter how much HR experience you have!

With this book, you now have a proven set of best practices and solutions for each stage of the process of moving into your new role and a comprehensive, specific game plan that will help you successfully navigate through your first 100 days in a new position.

You'll want to keep this guide with you for your entire HR career.

It will serve as your personal coach to ensure that each time you change HR jobs, you can start quickly, hit the ground running and take charge.

I wish you much success!

Onward!

Alan Collins

Alan L. Collins
Founder, Success in HR

P. S. If you're interested in more strategies and tactics for career success in HR, **CONNECT WITH US ONLINE.**

Subscribe to our Newsletter:
SuccessInHR.com

Connect with us on LinkedIn:
LinkedIn.com/in/SuccessInHR

Follow us on Facebook:
Facebook.com/SuccessinHRDaily

Follow us on Twitter:
@SuccessInHR

* * *

THE BRYAN A. COLLINS
SCHOLARSHIP PROGRAM

The Bryan A. Collins Memorial Scholarship Program awards scholarship grants every year to minority students who demonstrate excellence in pursuit of their college degrees.

Students selected for this scholarship must embody the values embraced by the late Bryan A. Collins -- great with people, great at academics, and great in extra-curricular leadership activities.

Bryan Collins was a rising star and well-respected student leader at Tennessee State University. Bryan received his B.S. degree in Biology from TSU in May 2005. At the time of his passing, he was enrolled in the Master's program in physical therapy and anxiously looking forward to commencing his doctoral studies. On campus, he was a leader in the Kappa Alpha Psi fraternity, served on the Civic Committee, the Community Service Committee, and help set strategic direction as a Board Member of the fraternity.

In addition, he found much success outside the classroom. He was voted Mr. Tennessee State first runner-up, was involved in the Student Union Board of Governors, was a founding member of the Generation of Educated Men, and worked closely with the Tennessee State University dean of admissions and records.

Bryan found comfort and relaxation in sports, music, movies, video games, friends, good parties, and just spending time with his family relaxing at home.

Key contributors to Bryan's scholarship program include the PepsiCo Foundation, the Motorola Foundation, Pamela Hewitt = Warren Lawson of Chicago and many other organizations and individuals. Additional details about Bryan, the scholarship program and how to contribute can be found at the scholarship website at BryanCollinsScholarship.org.

ABOUT THE AUTHOR

Alan Collins is the **Founder of Success in HR,** a company dedicated to empowering HR professionals and executives around the globe with insights and tools for enhancing their careers.

He currently serves 14,000+ HR subscribers through his flagship newsletter, "Success in HR" at SuccessInHR.com, and inspires countless others through his books, presentations, and coaching.

Alan was formerly Vice President of Human Resources at PepsiCo, where he led HR initiatives for their North American Quaker Oats, Gatorade, and Tropicana businesses. With 25 years as an HR executive and professional, Alan's corporate and operating human resources experience is extensive. He led an organization of 60 HR directors, managers, and professionals spread across 21 locations in North America, where he was accountable for their performance, careers, and success. In addition, he and his team provided HR strategic and execution oversight for a workforce of over 7000 employees, supporting $8 billion in sales. Alan also served as the HR M&A lead in integrating new acquisitions and divesting existing businesses; he provided HR leadership for one of the most significant change initiatives in the history of the PepsiCo organization.

Alan is the author of *Unwritten HR Rules* and *Stay Inspired in HR.* Both have been consistently ranked among Amazon's best-selling books for HR professionals. In addition, he has written over 100 articles and special reports on HR that have appeared in *HR Executive Magazine, HRM Today,* and other national publications for human resources professionals. He has also taught at various Chicago-area universities.

He received his B.S. degree in Management and M.S. in Industrial Relations & Human Resources from Purdue. More about Alan and his works can be found at SuccessInHR.com.